WALKING IN
THE THAMES VALLEY

About the Author

Steve Davison is a freelance writer and photographer and has lived in Berkshire for the past 20 years. He has written for a number of outdoor magazines and other publications including local and national newspapers, specialising in hillwalking and European travel, with interests in nature, geology and the countryside. A keen hillwalker for many years and holder of a Mountain Leader (summer) Certificate, Steve has also worked as a part-time outdoor education instructor. He is a member of the Outdoor Writers and Photographers Guild.

WALKING IN
THE THAMES VALLEY

by
Steve Davison

CICERONE

2 POLICE SQUARE, MILNTHORPE, CUMBRIA LA7 7PY
www.cicerone.co.uk

© Steve Davison 2008
First published 2008
ISBN-13: 978 1 85284 570 4

All photographs by the author.

A catalogue record for this book is available from the British Library.

o s Ordnance This project includes mapping data licensed from Ordnance
Survey® with the permission of the Controller of Her Majesty's
Stationery Office. © Crown copyright 2002. All rights reserved.
Licence number PU100012932

Advice to Readers

Readers are advised that while every effort is taken by the author to ensure the accuracy of this guidebook, changes can occur which may affect the contents. It is advisable to check locally on such things as transport, accommodation and shops but even rights of way can be altered.

The pu~~blisher~~ ~~would be~~ ~~notes of any such changes~~

Front cover: All Saints Church, Cuddesdon (Walk 19)

CONTENTS

INTRODUCTION...11
Getting Around...14
Food and Drink 15
Accommodation 15
When to Walk 15
Kit Suggestions...16
Walking with Children..16
Using the Guide..16
Maps 19
Access and Rights of Way 20
Long-Distance Routes...20

THE WALKS
Walk 1   Lechlade and a Thames Meander 24
Walk 2   Wiltshire Ridges and Liddington Castle 33
Walk 3   The Bedwyns 41
Walk 4   Fosbury Hill and the Chutes 51
Walk 5   Faringdon's Folly 59
Walk 6   Lambourn Downs: Striding out with horses and dragons...65
Walk 7   Thames Village Meander 77
Walk 8   Hanging Around on Walbury Hill 84
Walk 9   The Letcombe Gallop..90
Walk 10 Wantage and the Village Challenge 98
Walk 11 Farnborough: A poet's hideaway......................................107
Walk 12 Cold Ash and Hermitage: A writer's retreat.....................113
Walk 13 Blewbury and its Hillfort 121
Walk 14 Watership Down: A land of rabbits 131
Walk 15 The Pang Valley: A river runs through it 138
Walk 16 Dorchester-on-Thames: An ancient place of worship......148
Walk 17 The Aldworth Giants and Thurle Down 156
Walk 18 The Goring Challenge 164
Walk 19 Oxford Hills and the River Thame 173
Walk 20 Historic Ewelme and Swyncombe.....................................183
Walk 21 Roman around Silchester 190
Walk 22 Chiltern Patchwork...198
Walk 23 Thames and Chilterns Meander..206

Walk 24 Hambledon Valley and a Royal Regatta..214
Walk 25 Cookham and Stanley Spencer..221

APPENDIX 1 A Brief History.. 229
APPENDIX 2 Local Geology..231
APPENDIX 3 Useful Contacts 233
APPENDIX 4 Further Reading..235

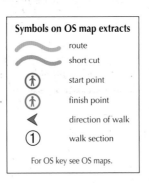

Symbols on OS map extracts

≈	route
≈	short cut
🚶	start point
🚶	finish point
◀	direction of walk
①	walk section

For OS key see OS maps.

Location of walls

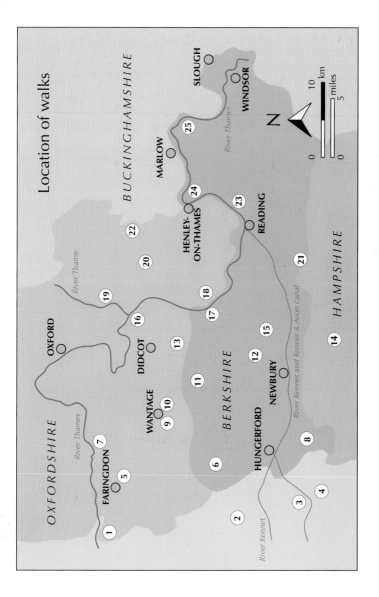

TABLE OF WALKS

	OS/Explorer map(s)	Start	Distance km/miles	Time hrs	Grade	Page
1 Lechlade and a Thames Meander	170	SU215995	24.1/15	6	1	24
Shorter option:			*12.8/8*	4		
2 Wiltshire Ridges and Liddington Castle	157	SU230786	18.5/11½	5	2	33
3 The Bedwyns	157&158	SU281644	20.9/13	5½	2	41
Shorter option:			*15.3/9½*	4		
4 Fosbury Hill and the Chutes	131	SU291582	20.9/13	6	3	51
Shorter option:			*16.1/10*	4½		
5 Faringdon's Folly	170	SU289956	19.3/12	5	2	59
Shorter option:			*11.3/7*	3¾		
6 Lambourn Downs: Striding out with horses and dragons	158&170	SU325789	*Day 1 17.7/11*	*Day 1* 5	3	65
			Day 2 24.1/15	*Day 2* 6½		
Shorter 1-day option:			29/18	8		
7 Thames Village Meander	170&180	SU345980	19.3/12	5	1	77
Shorter option:			*16.5/10¼*	4¾		
8 Hanging Around on Walbury Hill	158&131	SU370621	19.3/12	5½	3	84
9 The Letcombe Gallop	170	SU398879	20.1/12½	5½	2	90
10 Wantage and the Village Challenge	170	SU398879	24.9/15½	6½	2	98
11 Farnborough: A poet's hideaway	170	SU479840	19.3/12	5½	2	107
12 Cold Ash and Hermitage: A writer's retreat	158	SU505730	16.9/10½	4½	1	113

13	Blewbury and its Hillfort	170	SU584861	20.9/13	5½	1	121
14	Watership Down: A land of rabbits	144	SU527586	22.9/14¼	6½	3	131
	Shorter option:			*13.7/8½*	*4*		
15	The Pang Valley: A river runs through it	159	SU571697	20.1/12½	5¼	1	138
	Shorter option:			*13.7/8½*	*3¾*		
16	Dorchester-on-Thames: An ancient place of worship	170	SU567924	17.7/11	4¾	1	148
17	The Aldworth Giants and Thurle Down	159&170	SU583807	20.1/12½	5½	2	156
18	The Goring Challenge	171	SU599807	25.7/16	6¾	2	164
	Shorter option:			*13.7/8½*	*4*		
19	Oxford Hills and the River Thame	170&180	SU604988	20.1/12½	5½	2	173
20	Historic Ewelme and Swyncombe	171	SU648912	22.1/13¾	6	3	183
	Shorter option:			*11.5/7¼*	*3*		
21	Roman around Silchester	159	SU672642	17.7/11	4½	1	190
22	Chiltern Patchwork	171	SU710936	22.9/14¼	6¾	3	198
23	Thames and Chilterns Meander	171	SU757755	24.1/15	6¼	2	206
24	Hambleden Valley and a Royal Regatta	171	SU765822	21.7/13½	5½	1	214
25	Cookham and Stanley Spencer	172	SU892853	23.3/14½	6	1	221
	Shorter option:			*14.5/9*	*3¾*		

The route times are based on a walking speed of 2½mph or 4kmph, plus 10 minutes per 100m (300ft) of ascent and do not include any time for rests, lunch, photos, reading the map or simply enjoying the view – all of which can add substantially to the overall time. Always remember to walk at the pace of the slowest group member.

Simple indication as to the terrain (amount of ascent) covered during the walk

1 Low level: Less than 150m of ascent; 2 Moderate: 150–300m of ascent; 3 Hilly: More than 300m of ascent

The River Thames at Lechlade (Walk 1)

INTRODUCTION

This guidebook offers a collection of 25 adventurous circular walks in the Thames Valley, covering the Southern Chilterns, Berkshire, Lambourn and North Hampshire Downs and Southern Oxfordshire, all within easy reach of places such as Reading, Swindon, Newbury, Abingdon and surrounding towns.

All the walks – which vary in length from 10 to 18 miles (16 to 29km) and include a two-day (26-mile/42km) weekend walk over the Lambourn Downs – have a detailed route description that includes information on points of interest along the way, and are accompanied by a map based on Ordnance Survey Landranger 1:50,000 series maps. Many of the routes also have shorter (around 7–10-mile/11–16km) options, for those times when you want a less strenuous day out.

Some of the walks visit the ancient sites of Iron Age hillforts while others pass more modern features such as Wilton Windmill and the Kennet and Avon Canal. Many pass through picturesque villages with cosy pubs, thatched cottages and fascinating old churches. Some follow sections of the Ridgeway National Trail, which links some of the oldest 'green' roads in Britain, while others meander gently along the banks of the River Thames following the Thames Path. All the walks have one thing in common: they introduce the adventurous rambler to some of the best parts of the region.

The countryside encountered on these walks forms a patchwork of open chalk grassland, broadleaved woodland and farmland. Below the downs, chalk streams flow from the springline and support a diversity of plant and animal life; some of these streams, known as winterbournes, are seasonal and only appear during the wetter winter months. The richly wooded character of the Chiltern Hills distinguishes them from other, commonly more open, chalk landscapes such as the Lambourn Downs. Many of these woodlands are termed as ancient woodlands, defined as being continuously wooded since at least 1600. These areas tend to support a greater number of species and their

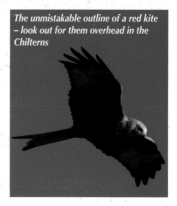

The unmistakable outline of a red kite – look out for them overhead in the Chilterns

character often closely reflects the underlying soil conditions, producing a wide range of woodland types and wildlife habitats.

You should have plenty of opportunities for catching glimpses of local wildlife, from foxes to roe and fallow deer or the much smaller muntjac; you may even be lucky enough to catch a glimpse of the elusive badger as dusk approaches. Along the riverbanks you may see herons patiently waiting for a fish to swim past, or the vivid turquoise-blue and orange flash of a kingfisher as it darts along the river, while the ever-present ducks, coots, moorhens and mute swans will keep you company.

As you wander through the ancient broadleaved beech and oak woodlands you may hear the drumming knock of the great spotted woodpecker declaring its territory, or the raucous call of a jay. Oak woods offer the more diverse wildlife habitat. Beech woods – a celebrated feature of the Chilterns – have a much denser canopy that greatly reduces the light reaching the ground, though even here, in late spring, the forest floor is carpeted with vivid bluebells.

The open chalk grasslands support rare butterflies, plants including gentians and orchids and traditional farmland birds such as the colourful pheasant; high above you'll often hear the skylark singing, or see the majestic silhouette of a buzzard soaring overhead. One of the success stories of the area is the reintroduction of the impressive red kite, and you'd be unlucky not to see one while walking in the Chilterns. These birds of prey, with distinctive forked tail, chestnut-

The River Thames at Sonning (Walk 23)

The view east from Haydown Hill (Walk 4)

red plumage and high-pitched whistling calls – 'weeoo-wee-wee-wee' – were driven to extinction by the end of the 19th century. However, in the early 1990s the RSPB and English Nature reintroduced some birds; their numbers have increased, and there are now over 200 pairs of breeding birds in the region.

The area is also home to two Areas of Outstanding Natural Beauty (AONB): the Chilterns and the North Wessex Downs. The aim of the AONB status is to conserve the natural beauty of the area and protect the landscape for future generations.

The Chilterns AONB was designated in 1965 and covers over 830 square kilometres of the beautiful Chiltern Hills, which stretch from Oxfordshire and the Thames Valley northeast through Buckinghamshire and Bedfordshire to Hitchin in Hertfordshire: an unspoilt area of rolling chalk hills, swathed in beech woods, quiet valleys and picturesque villages with characteristic brick-and-flint cottages (www.chilternsaonb.org).

The North Wessex Downs AONB, the third-largest in the country, covers a rural landscape that encompasses large areas of typical downland scenery from the Marlborough Downs to Watership Down, and includes the World Heritage Site at Avebury and the famous Uffington White Horse. The market towns of Marlborough and Hungerford can be found within its boundaries, as can large stretches of the Ridgeway National Trail and the Kennet and Avon Canal (www.northwessexdowns.org.uk).

A brief history and a guide to the geology of the region are given in Appendices 1 and 2.

GETTING AROUND

By car

The area enjoys a good road network with the M4 motorway running east–west and a number of main A-roads, such as the A34, travelling north–south. If you are travelling by car to the start of these walks please use designated parking areas and make sure you don't block access for local people and farmers.

By rail and bus

The main railway from London to the west gives access to some of the walks, while more local connecting services reach the likes of Henley-on-Thames and Cookham. Throughout the region several bus operators provide reasonably frequent services to several of the towns and villages and some of the walks, though not necessarily to the starting points. Bus services tend to be rather infrequent or non-existent on Sundays.

Brief details of bus and train services are given with each route description as appropriate. A good source of public transport maps for the Ridgeway and Thames Path is the National Trails website (www.nationaltrail.co.uk). These two maps cover many of the walks in this guidebook.

For rail service enquiries call National Rail Enquiries on 08457 484950 (www.nationalrail.co.uk). Information for planning a journey by bus, coach or train can be obtained by calling Traveline on 0871 200 22 33 (www.traveline.org.uk). Another service that may be useful is the Connect 2 Taxi (0871 750 0303) which automatically connects you to a cab service

The Rose Revived at Newbridge (Walk 7)

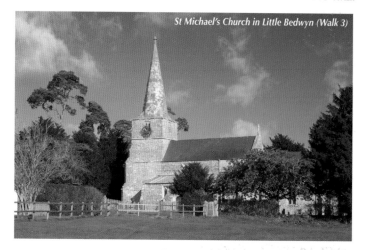

St Michael's Church in Little Bedwyn (Walk 3)

in your area. Contact details for bus companies operating in the region are given in Appendix 3.

FOOD AND DRINK

Most of the walks start near places where food and drink can be bought: a local shop, café or pub. Some offer opportunities for stopping off during the walk at a village with either a local shop or pub, although not always conveniently placed; brief details of villages with pubs, shops and cafés are given in the information box for each walk, though there is no guarantee that they'll be open when required. It's always a good idea to carry some food and drink with you, plus a small 'emergency ration' in case of an unexpected delay. Pubs or cafes passed en route are mentioned in the text.

ACCOMMODATION

There is a wide range of accommodation available from hotels to B&Bs and youth hostels. Contact the local tourist information office (see Appendix 3) for information on accommodation in a particular area.

WHEN TO WALK

Summers tend to be fairly dry and can be quite hot with hazy skies. Spring and autumn offer better walking conditions, with clearer skies making for better views. Cool autumn nights herald a dramatic change, with the trees – especially the Chiltern beech woods – becoming clothed in spectacular shades of russet, gold and brown, while in the early summer there are striking carpets of bluebells. During

15

A winter scene looking east to White Horse Hill on the Ridgeway (Walk 6)

the winter months spells of rain can make paths and tracks, especially on chalk-based soils, rather muddy, and rivers can flood surrounding fields, especially along the River Thames, making some routes impassable. Even though the days are quite short, walking on a clear, frosty, winter's day can be a magical experience and you maybe lucky enough to have rare fall of snow, especially on the higher downs.

KIT SUGGESTIONS

A good pair of walking boots, a comfortable rucksack, waterproof jacket and appropriate clothing for the time of year are necessities; on wet days, gaiters can also be very useful. Stinging nettles, which reach their peak during the summer, can be a problem on some of the walks, so

shorts are not always a good idea. It's also worth carrying a basic first aid kit to deal with minor incidents.

WALKING WITH CHILDREN

The walks are all fairly long and, although the terrain is not too hilly, they can be quite strenuous. Only older children who are used to longer walks should attempt these routes (note that 10 of the walks do have shorter options).

USING THE GUIDE

The walk descriptions in this guidebook all follow the same format. The individual route information section is followed by a brief guide to the walk, identifying any major points (including towns and villages). The information section gives the total length of

Beech trees in winter, Stonor Park (Walk 22)

THE COUNTRYSIDE CODE

While you are out enjoying these walks please respect the countryside and follow the Countryside Code.

Be safe – plan ahead and follow any signs

Even when going out locally, it's best to get the latest information about where and when you can go; for example, your rights to go onto some areas of open land may be restricted while work is carried out, for safety reasons or during bird breeding seasons. Follow advice and local signs, and be prepared for the unexpected.

Leave gates and property as you find them

Please respect the working life of the countryside, as our actions can affect people's livelihoods, our heritage, and the safety and welfare of animals and ourselves.

Protect plants and animals, and take your litter home

We have a responsibility to protect our countryside now and for future generations, so make sure you don't harm animals, birds, plants or trees.

Keep dogs under close control

The countryside is a great place to exercise dogs, but it's every owner's duty to make sure their dog is not a danger or nuisance to farm animals, wildlife or other people.

Consider other people

Showing consideration and respect for other people makes the countryside a pleasant environment for everyone – at home, at work and at leisure.

For further information visit www.countrysideaccess.gov.uk or call 0845 1003298.

the walk in miles and kilometres, the starting point, car parking, maps, public transport, distance and pubs. The walking times are based on a walking speed of 2½mph or 4kmph, plus 10 minutes per 100m (300ft) of ascent. This should be treated as the guide to the minimum walking time required to undertake the route and does not include time for rests, photography, consulting the map or guidebook, or simply admiring the view – all of which can add substantially to the day's activity. Always remember to pace the walk to the slowest member in the group, so that everyone can enjoy the day. There is also a simple indication as to the amount of ascent covered during the walk (see Table of Walks on pages 8 and 9).

The walks are split into numbered sections. The numbers, accompanied by grid references, correspond to the numbers highlighted on the route maps and will enable you to identify your location easily. The grid references are generated from the National Grid; each Ordnance Survey map is divided by a series of vertical and horizontal lines to create a grid with a spacing of 1km. You can locate a point on a map, accurate to within 100m, using a grid reference which is made up of two letters and six numbers.

The two letters correspond to the 100,000m^2 in which the grid reference lies, and can be found in the corners of any Ordnance Survey map. The first two digits of the six-figure number correspond to the vertical line (easting) to the left of the point of interest, using the horizontal numbers along the bottom and top of the map; the third digit is the tenths of the square (equivalent to 100m). Next find the fourth and fifth digits: locate the horizontal line (northing) below the point of interest. The last digit is again the number of tenths moving up through the square. Always remember – read the horizontal numbers before the vertical ones.

Throughout the route text you will find various easily identifiable items or places of interest highlighted in bold type; additional information is given for the latter.

Useful contact details are given in Appendix 3, and a Table of Walks on pages 8 and 9.

MAPS

Extracts from the Ordnance Survey Landranger series of maps, at a scale of 1:50,000, are used throughout this guidebook, with overlays showing the routes. However, these maps do not give the same level of detail and clarity as that found on the Ordnance Survey Explorer series, at a scale of 1:25,000 – for example, the location of a path in relation to field boundaries. For this reason walkers may find the larger scale mapping of value on some of the routes. Details of the relevant maps are given with each route description. The Explorer maps that cover the walks in this guidebook are:

- Explorer 157 Marlborough and Savernake Forest
- Explorer 158 Newbury and Hungerford
- Explorer 159 Reading, Wokingham and Pangbourne
- Explorer 170 Abingdon, Wantage and Vale of White Horse
- Explorer 171 Chiltern Hills West, Henley-on-Thames and Wallingford
- Explorer 172 Chiltern Hills East, High Wycombe, Maidenhead and Rickmansworth
- Explorer 180 Oxford, Witney and Woodstock

ACCESS AND RIGHTS OF WAY

All the walks suggested follow public rights of way, whether they be footpaths, bridleways or byways; some sections also follow permissive paths

Footpath sign at Radcot (Walk 1)

(routes where the landowner has allowed the public to have walking access). Paths are mostly well signed, but not always: in these cases care is required not to lose the way. Local authorities have a duty to protect and maintain the extensive network of off-road routes. Where a path is obstructed, you are entitled to divert around the obstruction. Please report any problems while using the rights of way mentioned in this guidebook to the relevant local authority.

In October 2005 the Countryside and Rights of Way (CROW) Act 2000 was completed, giving all users of the countryside the opportunity to walk freely across mapped 'access land' without the need to follow designated paths. Open access land includes mountain, moor, heath, down and registered common land, and these open access areas are marked by a yellow tint on the more recent Ordnance Survey Explorer maps.

20

Rights of way are marked on the ground as follows:
- **Footpath** Yellow arrow – walkers only
- **Bridleway** Blue arrow – walkers, cyclists and horse riders
- **Byway** Red arrow – walkers, cyclists, horse riders, motorcycles and vehicles
- **Restricted Byway** Purple arrow – use by all except mechanically propelled vehicles, but can be narrow and so may not take, for example, a horse and cart.

LONG-DISTANCE ROUTES

If you fancy a longer and more testing walk several long-distance routes pass through the Thames Valley, and all of them are visited by at least one of the walks described in this book.

Chiltern Way (Walk 20)

The Chiltern Way was created by the Chiltern Society as its Millennium project (officially launched in October 2000), and is based on an earlier unofficial route, the Chiltern Hundred (100 miles/161km). The route takes in four counties: Bedfordshire, Buckinghamshire, Hertfordshire and Oxfordshire, in a 133-mile (214km) circuit (extended to 172 miles in 2003) from Ewelme in the southwest to Sharpenhoe Clappers and Great Offley in the northeast, and as far southeast as Chorleywood West.

Looking across to the Devil's Punchbowl from the Ridgeway (Walk 9)

D'Arcy Dalton Way (Walk 1)
The D'Arcy Dalton Way is a 66-mile (106km) north–south path between Wormleighton near Banbury and Wayland's Smithy on the Ridgeway. The route was created to mark the Oxford Fieldpath Society's Diamond Jubilee in 1986 and was named after a notable defender of the county's path network. The route passes through parts of the Cotswolds, Thames Valley, Vale of the White Horse and Wessex Downs.

Lambourn Valley Way (Walk 6)
The Lambourn Valley Way is a 22-mile (35km) walk running from the Berkshire Downs at the Uffington White Horse to Newbury, following the picturesque valley of the River Lambourn.

Oxfordshire Way (Walk 22)
The Oxfordshire Way is a 65-mile (104km) lowland path linking the Cotswolds at Bourton-on-the-Water with the Chilterns and River Thames at Henley-on-Thames. The route passes through the most rural and scenic landscapes of Oxfordshire, including two AONBs: the Cotswolds, with their characteristic grey limestone buildings and stone walls and the Chilterns, with their flint-and-brick architecture and famous beech woods.

Ridgeway National Trail (Walks 2, 6, 9, 10, 11, 17 and 20)
The Ridgeway, designated as a long-distance route in 1972, stretches for 85 miles (137km) across five counties, from Overton Hill near Avebury in Wiltshire to Ivinghoe Beacon in Buckinghamshire. However, it is just part of a prehistoric track that once stretched for 248 miles (400km) from the Dorset coast to the Wash on the Norfolk coast. Its purpose was to provide a route for travellers over high

21

ground which was less wooded and drier than routes following the springline villages below. These ancient trackways have been in use for over 5000 years, making them some of the oldest roads in Britain.

Along the Ridgeway, man has left evidence of early occupation in the form of Neolithic and Bronze Age burial mounds and later Iron Age hillforts. Three hillforts along the western section of the Ridgeway are visited on separate walks detailed in this book. These are Liddington Castle (Walk 2), Uffington Castle (Walk 6) and Segsbury or Letcombe Castle (Walks 6 and 10). The atmospheric Neolithic burial mound at Wayland's Smithy and the stunning Uffington White Horse, believed to be 3000 years old, are visited on Walk 6.

Shakespeare Way (Walk 19)

This long-distance path, following minor roads and footpaths, runs for 146 miles (235km) between Stratford-upon-Avon – Shakespeare's birthplace –and Shakespeare's Globe Theatre in London.

Swan's Way (Walk 20)

A long-distance bridle route of 65 miles (105km) from the River Thames at Goring in the south to Salcey Forest in Northamptonshire, passing through a variety of Buckinghamshire landscapes en route.

Thames Path (Walks 1, 7, 16, 18, 23, 24 and 25)

The National Trail, opened in 1996, follows England's best-known river for 184 miles (294km) as it meanders from its source in the Cotswolds near Kemble (Gloucestershire) through the bustle of London to the Thames Barrier in Woolwich. En route the path passes through several rural counties and fascinating urban areas such as Oxford, Henley-on-Thames, Windsor and Greenwich, as well as peaceful water meadows rich in wildlife. A 10-mile (16km) extension from the Thames Barrier east to the Crayford Ness marshes was added in 2001.

Test Way (Walk 8)

A 44-mile (71km) route starting on the chalk downs at Inkpen Beacon where the Wayfarer's Walk ends (see below). The route follows much of the course of the River Test, passing through some of Hampshire's picturesque villages, to reach the coast at Southampton Water.

Wayfarer's Walk (Walks 8 and 14)

The Wayfarer's Walk stretches for 70 miles (113km) through Hampshire from the coast near Portsmouth to Inkpen Beacon just across the Berkshire border, where it meets the Test Way. The Wayfarer's Walk provides a fine selection of walking terrain from coastal to gentle rolling hills, dotted with the dense woodland and rich green valleys for which Hampshire is renowned.

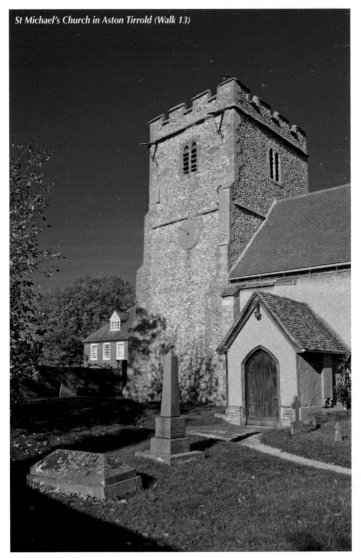

St Michael's Church in Aston Tirrold (Walk 13)

WALK 1

Lechlade and a Thames Meander

Distance	15 miles (24.1km) or 8 miles (12.8km)
Time	6 hours or 4 hours
Grade	1
Map	OS Explorer 170/Landranger 163
Start/finish	Market Place next to St Lawrence's Church in Lechlade (SU215995); parking at Memorial Hall and sports ground along Burford Street (A361) (SU214998)
Public transport	Bus links to Swindon and Cirencester
Refreshments	Lechlade – several pubs, café and shops; Buscot – tea room in village shop; Radcot – Swan Hotel (01367 810220); Kelmscott – The Plough Inn (01367 253543); St John's Lock – The Trout Inn (01367 252313)

The walk starts from the town of Lechlade on Thames and follows the Thames upstream to the hamlet of Inglesham with its unspoilt church before heading off towards Buscot; a short detour can be made to visit the village (owned by the National Trust, with small shop and café). On reaching the Thames south of Kelmscott a decision has to be made: short or long route? The short walk heads back along the River Thames, while the long walk heads off through farmland passing the hamlet of Eaton Hastings to reach Radcot and the oldest bridge over the Thames. From here the walk follows the meandering Thames Path back to Lechlade with a short excursion through the village of Kelmscott, passing the former home of William Morris.

A long circular walk through three counties which can be shortened by missing out Radcot and Kelmscott.

Lechlade-on-Thames, on the edge of the Cotswolds, is dominated by the fine 15th-century St Lawrence's Church (there is evidence of a 13th-century church on the same site). The Perpendicular-style church, decorated with gargoyles and grotesque sculptures, is built of local stone from Taynton Quarry near Burford, which also supplied the stone for St Paul's Cathedral in London. Inside there are some good memorial brasses,

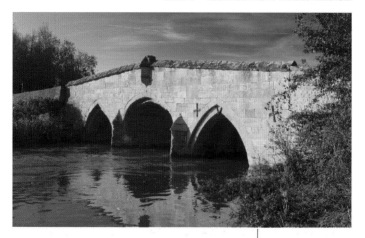

The oldest bridge on the Thames, at Radcot

including one to local wool merchant John Townsend (d. 1458) and his wife Ellen. One of the best features is the 15th-century chancel roof. Only fragments of the earlier church remain, including two stone plaques, one of which depicts the martyrdom of St Agatha.

The late author and architectural historian, David Verey, described the parish church as 'One of the six finest churches in Gloucestershire', while in 1815 the great English Romantic poet Percy Bysshe Shelley (1792–1827) was inspired to write about the church in his 'Stanzas in Lechlade Churchyard':

> *Thou too, aereal Pile! Whose pinnacles*
> *Point from one shrine like pyramids of fire*
> *Obeyist in silence their sweet solemn spells,*
> *Clothing in hues of Heaven thy dim and distant*
> *   spire*
> *Around whose lessening and invisible height*
> *Gather among the stars the clouds of night.*

At the bottom of Bell Lane, off the High Street, is the site of the old wharf and the point at which the river was crossed by means of Tidford ford, in use until

Ha'penny Bridge was built in 1792. The bridge is named after the amount of toll levied to cross; the toll-house still stands on the bridge and forms part of the eastern parapet.

① **SU215995** From the Market Place go west along the High Street and then left into Thames Street (A361) to cross over **Ha'penny Bridge**. Immediately turn right following the Thames Path, later passing the confluence of the River Coln and the point where the disused Thames and Severn Canal joined the Thames. The **Round House** on the opposite bank was built to accommodate the lock-keepers and is one of several along the route of the canal.

The **Thames and Severn Canal** was built in the 1780s to connect with the Stroudwater Navigation, built a few years earlier, thereby linking the Rivers Thames and Severn – the first inland waterway route between London and the Midlands. However, the opening of

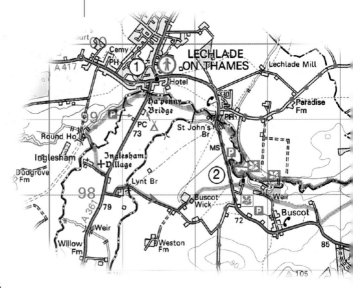

the Kennet and Avon Canal captured most of the Bristol trade and the coming of the railways in the mid-1840s started a slow decline in trade; the last boat travelled along the canal in 1911. The Cotswold Canals Trust is working to re-open the canal.

Cross the footbridge and follow the path away from the river towards **Inglesham**, cross the stile to join a tarred lane; to the right is the interesting **Church of St John the Baptist**.

Inglesham is Wiltshire's most northerly hamlet, and borders the counties of Gloucestershire and Oxfordshire. Although very small, the hamlet has two points of interest: St John the Baptist's Church and Inglesham Polo Club at Lynt Farm. The church, now cared for by the Churches Conservation Trust, may date back to late Saxon times, but has remained substantially unaltered since the early 1500s. Inside are

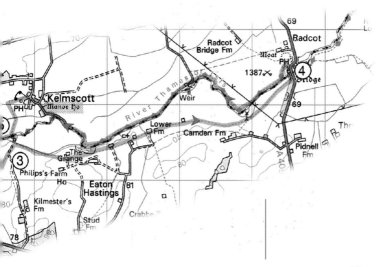

the original box pews, while a carving on the north wall of the Mother and Child is believed to be Saxon.

Turn left along the road (away from the church) and then right along the main road (A361). At the junction follow the lane left towards Buscot for ¼ mile (1.2km). Turn left towards **Buscot Wick Farm**, and after passing a small grassy area and tree, go right past a house. Follow the track round towards another house and take the gate on the right; keep to the left field boundary and follow the track past a new barn. Later head diagonally right across the field, passing to the left of a large oak tree. Go through a gate by another oak tree and follow the field edge. Turn left through a gate to diagonally cross the corner of the field to a gate and road (A417).

② **SU225981** Cross over and take the path opposite with **Buscot Parsonage** over to the left. Cross the stile at the far side of the field and turn left along the lane towards **St Mary's Church** in **Buscot**.

Buscot, formerly the most northwesterly village in Berkshire (now in Oxfordshire), is owned by the National Trust and can be visited by a short detour from Buscot Weir. However, the route does pass St Mary's Church, which is definitely worth a visit. The church, which dates from about 1200, has an interesting pulpit with wooden panels believed to have been painted by the early 16th-century Flemish artist Jan Gossaert (1478–1532), while two of the beautiful stained-glass windows are by the pre-Raphaelite artist Sir Edward Burne-Jones.

Bear right through the churchyard and leave via the lych-gate. Continue across the field and through a kissing gate, then follow the enclosed path to reach a lane at **Buscot Weir**. Turn right, away from the river, for a short distance before heading left across the grass to the far right corner. Cross the footbridge and stile and continue with the field boundary on the right. At the corner go right and left into the next field, with the field edge and

St Mary's Church at Buscot

house on the left; keep ahead and cross the stile next to
the gate to go right along the track (byway) towards the
A417. Just before the road turn left through a gate and
walk diagonally across the field. Keep ahead through a
gap in the hedge, cross the footbridge and follow the
path right and left before going over a gentle rise, keeping the hedge on the left. On reaching a large footpath
sign, bear diagonally left over the field and along the
track towards the river, passing through a gate.

Shorter walk
Follow the path round the right-hand side of a building to cross over the river via the bridge and turn left
along the Thames Path (see Point 5) back to Lechlade
and the Ha'penny Bridge.

③ **SU247985** Before reaching the river, cross the stile in
the fence on the right and follow the left field edge;

continue through several fields. Cross a footbridge to the left of The Grange and later a concrete track leading to Rhodes Farm. Continue over the footbridge and field to reach a stile and tarred lane. Keep ahead, passing **St Michael's and All Angels Church** in **Eaton Hastings**; the route is now following part of the D'Arcy Dalton Way.

> Although today a parish of scattered settlements, **Eaton Hastings** was once a thriving village. The name derives from the Anglo-Saxon word *tun*, meaning 'homestead or village by a river'; 'Hastings' derives from Ralph de Hastings who held the manor in the 12th century. The Norman church of St Michael's and All Angels, around which the village was centred, sits close to the south bank of the Thames.

Shortly after passing the church, go through the small gate just to the right of the house driveway and keep close to the fence before continuing over the field. Cross the stile, footbridge and track leading to **Lower Farm**, go over the stile in the fence opposite next to the wooden pole and follow the fence on the left. Continue across the open field, aiming for the small gate in the hedge to the left of the larger gate. Cross the footbridge and go through another gate to keep ahead past an area of scrub on the left. After the next field cross stiles either end of a footbridge, and continue through three more fields, crossing at stiles and passing **Camden Farm** over to the right, to reach a small old windmill. Continue past the pond, cross a stile and follow the left field edge; cross another stile and pass to the right of a large pylon. Keep ahead through the field, and at the field corner cross a stone stile to join the road (A4095).

> **Radcot** boasts the original three-arched bridge, claimed to the oldest bridge on the Thames. The smaller single-spanned bridge, closest to the Swan Hotel, was built in 1787 along with the new river cutting and takes the river traffic.

④ **SU286994** Turn left towards **Radcot** and after crossing the second bridge the Swan Hotel is to the right; turn left through the gate along the Thames Path, signposted 'D'Arcy Dalton Way and Kelmscott 3'. Continue along the riverside path for about 3 miles (4.8km) and just before Kelmscott, where the Thames Path goes left off the gravel track, keep ahead along the track towards the village, later joining a tarred lane. Go past the entrance to **Kelmscott Manor** and at the split bear left to reach **The Plough Inn**.

Kelmscott is famed for its connections with the founder of the Arts and Crafts Movement, William Morris (1834–96). The pre-Raphaelite designer, interior decorator, writer and painter is best remembered for his still-popular furnishing designs, rich with flowers, leaves and birds. Morris worked with other great pre-Raphaelite artists such as Edward Burne-Jones and Dante Gabriel Rossetti.

Kelmscott Manor, which dates from 1570, was bought by Morris in 1871 as his summer retreat and contains many examples of his work. The house, now owned by the Society of Antiquaries of London, is open on Wednesdays and some Saturdays through the summer (01367 252486 for details). When he moved to Kelmscott, Morris wrote:

> What better place than this, then, could we find,
> By this sweet stream that knows not of the sea,
> That guesses not of the city's misery,
> This little stream whose hamlets scarce have names,
> This far off, lonely mother of the Thames.

Morris is buried, with his wife and daughter, at Kelmscott's 12th-century St George's Church (short walk off-route).

Turn right and left following the lane round the pub, passing the stump of an old village cross. Take the enclosed footpath on the right of the house driveway and

Old Father Thames at St John's Lock

shortly turn left with the field boundary on the left through the next field, now with the fence on the right, to reach the river.

⑤ **SU247986** Turn right and continue along the Thames Path (**shorter walk rejoins here**), later passing **Buscot Lock**. Near St John's Bridge, ignore the alternative Thames Path that turns away from the river, but instead cross the river via the new bridge. Turn right following the left-hand riverbank under the bridge; **The Trout Inn** is on the far side of the river, accessible via the road bridge. Continue past **St John's Lock** and **Old Father Thames** statue, and immediately after **Ha'penny Bridge** turn left up to the road and cross the river, retracing the route back to the Market Place.

St John's Lock, the first lock on the river, is named after a medieval priory dedicated to St John the Baptist, built where the Trout Inn now stands. The first bridge over the river here was built in 1229, though the present structure is much more recent. Overlooking the lock is the recumbent figure of Old Father Thames, originally created for the 1851 Great Exhibition at Crystal Palace in London. The statue was later used to mark the source of the river before being moved to St John's Lock in 1974.

WALK 2

Wiltshire Ridges and Liddington Castle

Distance	11½ miles (18.5km)
Time	5 hours
Grade	2
Map	OS Explorer 157/Landranger 174
Start/finish	Parking at lay-by on B4192, 3 miles (4.8km) northwest of Aldbourne towards Liddington (SU230786)
Public transport	Thames Down buses between Swindon and Hungerford/Marlborough stop at Aldbourne
Refreshments	Aldbourne – The Blue Boar (01672 540237); Crown Hotel (01672 540214); Masons Arms (01672 540124); village shop

The walk starts out in rolling countryside, where the Berkshire Downs become the Marlborough Downs, and follows a broad ridge down to the picturesque village of Aldbourne with its village green, duck pond and thatched cottages.

The return leg passes the site of the village of Snap, deserted just over 100 years ago, and the Iron Age hillfort of Liddington Castle. The hillfort, with its commanding position on the highest hill along the Ridgeway National Trail, offers some great views. The area is also rich in Neolithic long barrows, and several can be seen during the walk.

① **SU230786** From the lay-by walk down the road for 100m towards **Aldbourne**, and turn left through the gate. Go along the track signed 'byway to Peaks Down', following the left-hand fence through a gate and continue uphill. Go through the gate next to the byway sign and follow the fence on the left. Just before the gate leading into the trees, turn right and follow the track signposted 'byway to Aldbourne 2', keeping the trees on the left. After about 500m there is a well-defined tumulus on the right.

This walk may also be started from Aldbourne (SU265756).

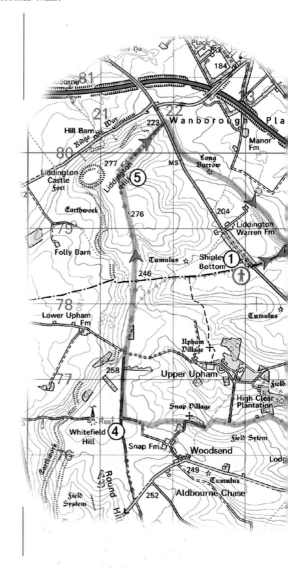

Continue along the track and through a gate to reach **Four Barrows** – a collection of Neolithic burial mounds.

Three of the **Four Barrows** are bell barrows, built with a gap between the mound and the ditch; the fourth barrow is a bowl barrow, shaped like an upturned bowl. These types of burial chamber are characteristic of the early Bronze Age (2300–1200BC). During archaeological excavations two skeletons and two cremations were found along with amber beads, a grooved dagger, a stone axe and flint arrowheads.

The track passes to the right of the first three and then goes left before the last one to reach a gate. The route now follows the track down the broad ridge for 1¼ miles (2km) to Aldbourne (*alternative start point*).

The name **Aldbourne** is derived from the Saxon word for stream – *bourne*, and a former local chief – *Ealda*. The interesting Church of St Michael, on the village green, was rebuilt in Gothic style but incorporates many Norman features from an earlier church. Inside there are some fine memorials, including one to Richard Goddard (d. 1492) and his wife Elizabeth of Upham House. There are also two old fire pumps, known locally as Adam and Eve. Originally bought after a disastrous fire in 1777 which damaged many houses, the pumps were last used for a barn fire in 1921.

The village has had several local trades including straw and willow weaving, though it was best known for its bell foundries. The first foundry was opened in 1694 by the Cor brothers, William and Robert. In 1760 a relation, Robert Wells, opened a second foundry which continued operating until the 1850s. It was once said that there were few places in north Wiltshire that were out of earshot of a bell cast in Aldbourne; the local church has three bells cast in the 18th century.

Interestingly, locals were once known as 'Aldbourne dabchicks'. The story goes that a dabchick arrived on the village pond but the local residents couldn't identify it; this amused the people of Ramsbury, who taunted their Aldbourne neighbours by shouting 'dabchick' after them!

In 1971 the village had a starring role in a *Dr Who* story when it was transformed into Devil's End, with The Blue Boar pub being renamed The Cloven Hoof. During the final episode a realistic model of the church was blown up.

② **SU264759** Turn right down the lane, ignoring the path off to the left, to reach The Green in **Aldbourne**, with the church off to the right. Continue down the lane past the **Blue Boar** pub. On reaching The Square, with the pond ahead, turn right past the Crown Hotel and then right along the B4192 for ¾ mile (1.2km) – take care on the road.

St Michael's Church in Aldbourne

Alternative route

To miss out the centre of the village go to the right passing the church and turn right up the lane next to the church wall. Just before the gate leading to the house, turn left along the signposted path between the wall and hedge. Continue past the school playground, cross the stile and across the field, keeping to the right of the buildings to reach a small gate in the fence; turn right along the B4192 to rejoin the route.

③ **SU255762** At **New Barn**, on the right, turn left along the farm track. After 200m take the left-hand track, signposted 'byway to Snap and Ridgeway', up the valley for about 2 miles (3.2km) passing **Lower Lodge Barn** on the way; the other track goes to Upper Upham. Not long after **High Clear Plantation**, ignore the track on the right and keep ahead through the field, following the boundary on the left. After 300m turn left uphill following the track as it bears to the right. On the right, at the bend, is a small memorial to Snap Toothill School and the remains of the village of **Snap**.

A small plaque reads 'In memory of the people of Snap Toothill School 5–8–1991'. All that remains of the village of **Snap** are a few piles of rubble hidden amongst the undergrowth and trees. The village, once part of the Aldbourne parish, dates back to at least 1377 when it was mentioned in connection with the Poll Tax. By the end of the 19th century the hamlet consisted of 15 houses, a school and chapel. However, with changes from labour-intensive arable farming to animal grazing, the residents had to move on to find work. By 1905 the village of Snap was abandoned except for the farm, though during World War I the area was used by the War Ministry as a training ground.

Continue, ignoring the paths to Woodsend and Snap Farm. Go through the gate and follow the track uphill, passing under the telegraph wires to another gate. Go straight on, passing between the fields for 300m to join the **Ridgeway National Trail**.

The Blue Boar pub in Aldbourne

④ **SU213765** Turn right along the track and, at the junction, follow the signs for the **Ridgeway** to the right for 50m and then left, with good views towards **Liddington Hill**. At the junction take the middle path – Ridgeway Path. After 350m go through the gate and then uphill, keeping close to the fence on the right. Once over the top of the hill, go through the gate next to some trees and continue across the field to another gate. On the left are the clearly defined earthworks of **Liddington Castle** hillfort.

Looking north from the ramparts of Liddington Castle

Detour

Although not on the main track, a detour can be made along a permissive path to **Liddington Castle**. At the gate, follow the path to the left, keeping to the fence on the right; at the field corner go left through a gate to follow the fence on your left. Go through another gate on the left to reach the hillfort, which offers some great views.

The remains of an Iron Age hillfort, one of several along the Ridgeway, crowns the summit of Liddington Hill – the highest point on the Ridgeway at 277m (910ft), with commanding views to the north. The fort, which is constructed of a single rampart and ditch with an entrance on the eastern side, was probably used after the Iron Age as Roman artefacts have been found in the area. Some claim this to be the site of the Battle of Mount Badon where the Britons, led by Arthur, defeated the Saxons.

Retrace your steps back to the gate on the Ridgeway path.

⑤ **SU212797** Go through the gate and follow the track down to the road (B4192); opposite is a sign for 'Sugar Hill 1½'. Cross the road and stile and turn right along the field edge, passing a large and small gate. The path follows the fence left and right to reach another gate. Keep to the track, with the fence on the right; to your right are the remains of a **Neolithic long barrow** or burial mound. Go through the gate and continue for 120m to another gate; keep straight on, with the fence on the right, and pass two more gates. Continue between two fenced fields, go through the gate and keep ahead across the field, with the fence on the right. At the gate, turn right down the hill and later turn right along the road back to the lay-by.

WALK 3
The Bedwyns

Distance	13 miles (20.9km) or 9½ miles (15.3km)
Time	5½ hours or 4 hours
Grade	2
Map	OS Explorers 157 and 158/Landranger 174
Start/finish	Great Bedwyn Wharf car park on east side of canal (SU281644)
Public transport	Trains to Great Bedwyn, bus links to Hungerford and Marlborough
Refreshments	Little Bedwyn – The Harrow Inn (01672 870871); Shalbourne – Plough Inn (01672 870295); Wilton – Swan Inn (01672 870274); Crofton – shop selling refreshments at museum (opening times only); Great Bedwyn – The Cross Keys (01672 870678); The Three Tuns (01672 870280)

A fairly level route starting out from Great Bedwyn and passing through both Little Bedwyn and Shalbourne before heading through the wooded country-side of Bedwyn Brail, a remnant of Savernake Forest, to reach the little village of Wilton. The return leg follows the Kennet and Avon Canal from Crofton, which runs parallel to the railway line from London to the Westcountry. During the walk there is the opportunity to look at Wilton Windmill and the Cornish beam engines at Crofton, both of which are open to the public.

The **Kennet and Avon Canal** was formed by the joining of two waterways in the early 19th century. The Kennet Navigation from the Thames at Reading to Newbury was built in 1724, and the Avon Navigation from Bath to Bristol was completed three years later. In 1794 an Act of Parliament authorising the building of the connection between Newbury and Bath received Royal Assent, and in 1810 the canal was completed. Transporting goods along the canal proved successful for 40 years until the

This walk can be shortened by missing out Wilton and Crofton.

completion of the railway, which offered a faster transport route. In 1852 the canal was bought by the Great Western Railway Company (GWR), and allowed to go into decline. By 1955 the canal was in poor condition, though plans to abandon it were stopped by public opposition. The canal has since been restored by the Kennet and Avon Canal Trust, and was reopened in 1990.

The railway running parallel to the canal is part of the line from Reading to the West Country. It was originally known as the Kennet Valley Line, designed by Isambard Kingdom Brunel, and operated by Berkshire and Hampshire Railways with backing from the GWR.

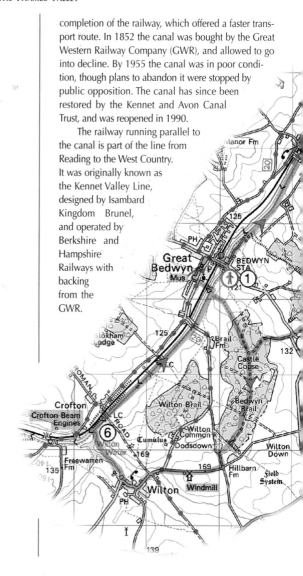

The section from Hungerford to Devizes only opened in 1862, but the section from Reading to Hungerford opened in 1847.

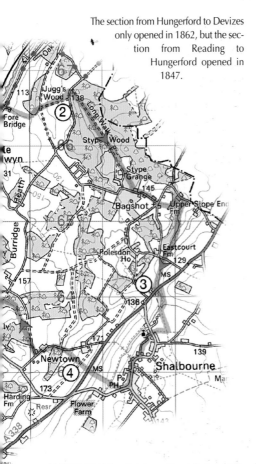

① **SU281644** Starting from **Great Bedwyn Wharf** car park, follow the Kennet and Avon Canal towpath under the bridge and towards **Little Bedwyn** for about 1¼ miles (2km). Cross over the canal and railway using the footbridge and turn right along the road; at the junction bear right towards **St Michael's Church**.

The Kennet and Avon Canal at Great Bedwyn

Little Bedwyn, a small village straddling the River Dun, Kennet and Avon Canal and the railway, was known as Estbedwinda in 1177 and Lyttelbedwyn in 1547. St Michael's Church dates from the 12th century, though most of what is seen today is 15th century with 19th-century alterations. Much of the village was built around 1860, just before the arrival of the railway.

Just before the churchyard, turn right through the kissing gate and follow the hedge round to the left, keeping the church on your left. Continue ahead through Sandy's Wood, cross the stile and follow the path along the right-hand field edge. Turn right at the field corner, cross the railway line (*with care*) and go over the canal. Continue straight on across the road following a gravel track, later a path, up past **Jugg's Cottage**. Keep to the slightly sunken path as it first climbs and then descends, bearing left round **Jugg's Wood**. At the track junction go straight over, heading eastwards up along the hedged bridleway.

② **SU305666** At the T-junction go left along the track, and shortly after the right-hand bend turn right over two stiles to follow a gravel track, **Long Walk**, gently uphill through **Stype Wood**. Shortly after passing a house on the right bear slightly left, away from the track, to reach a gate. Follow the white posts across the open field, keeping left of **Stype Grange**, and cross a stile in the field corner just right of some cottages to join a lane. Turn left and, at the junction, cross slightly to the left and follow a path over the field before bearing half-left through trees. Continue between the disused farm buildings and turn right along the lane for a short distance, and just after the last barn go right at the gate (overgrown stile). Follow the path, keeping close to the edge of **Westcott Copse** on the right and, at the end of the wood, keep ahead over the field to cross two stiles either side of a metalled drive. Follow the right-hand bank of the **River Shalbourne** and bear left at the junction, just before some buildings, to reach the road (A338).

③ **SU317641** Cross the road and turn left over the bridge, then right to follow a path along the left-hand bank of the river. At the overgrown stile in the field corner cross the footbridge and continue through the field with the ditch on the right. At the junction turn right over the field aiming for the church. Cross the stile and follow the drive past the house down to Mill Lane in **Shalbourne**; continue along the lane opposite, up towards **St Michael's Church**.

The name **Shalbourne** is derived from the Anglo-Saxon words *scealde burna* meaning 'shallow stream', and watercress was once grown here in the clear waters. The oldest part of St Michael's and All Angels Church is the nave with two 12th-century lancet windows and a Norman doorway. Inside there are several interesting monuments, including a plaque commemorating Jethro Tull (1674–1741). Tull, who was born at Basildon and lived at Prosperous Home Farm, was a pioneer of British agricultural reform and invented both the horse-drawn hoe and drilling machine, forerunner of the modern seed drill.

Turn left at the church along the fenced path to reach **Kingston Lane** next to a school. Go right along the road through the village, and bear right at the Y-junction along Burr Lane; the **Plough Inn** is ahead on the right. Immediately after the last house cross the stile on the right, and follow the right-hand field edge; cross another stile and footbridge at the far side of the field. Continue uphill to the right of the hedge and then go through a hedge gap to reach the road (A338).

④ **SU308631** Cross over and up the bank to follow a waymarked path over the field. Turn left along the concrete track passing the wood and bear left and right round the front of **Newtown Farm**, then left along the lane. Turn right along the metalled bridleway; ignore the bridleway off to the left, and continue ahead through the wood. Just after passing the open field on the left, turn left along the bridleway through the wood. On emerging from the trees, turn left along the field edge and at the corner go through the belt of trees and turn right along a path. Keep straight on to reach a field and then follow the edge of the pine plantation on your left downhill, bearing left. At the bottom of the field bear slightly right across the field to pass between the two stands of trees, and continue towards **Folly Farm**. Turn right along the lane (bridleway) to reach a road at a Y-junction.

⑤ **SU290635** Cross both roads and follow a path on the left-hand side of a stand of trees, with hedges/fences on either side. Keep to the path as it bears left into **Bedwyn Brail** woodland and reach a cross-tracks junction.

Bedwyn Brail Several places in the area bear the name 'brail', a word used to describe an enclosed park, or wood, stocked with deer; Bedwyn Brail was once part of the great hunting forest of Savernake. The brail is the site of a home that Edward Seymour, Warden of Savernake and Lord Protector 1547–49 in the reign of

Wilton Windmill built in 1821

Edward IV, was building at the time of his execution in 1552, and also of a former Roman villa; nothing remains of either.

Shorter walk

Turn right along the track and keep left at the split; leave the wood and follow the left field boundary. Later walk downhill and bear right to join the canal towpath beside a bridge, where you pick up the final section of the main walk.

To continue on the main walk, turn left along a well-defined track signposted to the windmill, ignoring any tracks off to right or left for about ¾ mile (1.2km). Go through the gate and turn half-right for about 40m to where the track splits; take the left-hand path, keeping close to the fence on the left. At the T-junction turn left along the track and then right along the road towards Wilton, passing Wilton Windmill on the left.

Wilton Windmill, which stands on a chalk ridge at 170m (550ft), was built in 1821 and is the oldest working mill in Wiltshire, still producing stoneground wholemeal flour (on sale). Built from brick, the mill has a fantail that keeps the sails aligned with the wind, acting as an automatic rudder. The mill is open from Easter until the end of September on Sundays and Bank Holiday Mondays 2–5pm (01672 870202).

Continue down to **Wilton** with its thatched-and-timber-framed cottages, and bear right past **The Swan Inn** along the road for Grafton and Burbage. Just before the left-hand bend, next to the duck pond, turn right for a few metres through the hedge gap and then left, following a track past **Wilton Water** to reach the canal.

Crofton Pump House on the Kennet and Avon Canal

Detour

Take a detour to visit the **Crofton Pump House Museum** (shop selling refreshments when open). Turn left and cross the canal via the lock gates, then follow the path under the railway and up the steps to the pump house, which was designed by John Rennie, the Kennet and Avon Canal company's chief engineer. The two Cornish beam engines, built in 1812 and 1846, are driven by steam from a hand-stoked coal-fired Lancashire boiler, making them two of the oldest working steam-driven pumps in the world. They were originally used to pump water up from Wilton Water (a small lake built in 1836) to the summit of the canal. After a considerable amount of restoration work, Crofton was officially reopened by Sir John Betjeman in 1970. The museum is open at weekends from Easter to October; on Bank Holidays one of the pumps is usually 'in steam' (01672 870300). Retrace your steps back across the canal to rejoin the route.

⑥ **SU263622** Follow the towpath northeast towards **Great Bedwyn** for 1½ miles (2.4km). On reaching Great

Bedwyn Bridge, just after passing Lock 64, leave the towpath and cross the bridge over the canal (**shorter walk rejoins here**). Go through the gates either side of the railway line (*care required*) to follow a path across the field and then along the side of the churchyard wall. Go over the V-stile on the right and continue past the **Church of St Mary the Virgin** and the well-preserved preaching cross.

In Saxon times **Great Bedwyn** was known as Bedanheaford – meaning 'the graves head' – and was the residence of the Saxon chief Cissa. By the time of the Domesday Book (1086) the town was known as Bedewinde and was held by the king. The Church of St Mary the Virgin (dating from 1092, though most of what is visible is from the 12th/13th centuries) is one of the largest in the area. Inside is an impressive monument to Sir John Seymour, father of Jane Seymour who married King Henry VIII in 1536. She died in 1537 shortly after the birth of their son, who later became Edward VI. The church also holds the stone figure of a knight, believed to be Sir Adam de Stokke (d. 1313), and the tomb of Sir Roger de Stokke (d. 1333), son of Sir Adam. Also in the village is Lloyd's Stonemason's Museum. Run by the descendants of Benjamin Lloyd, the original mason to the Kennet and Avon Canal Company, the museum traces the fascinating history of stonemasonry. The museum is open to members of the public during work hours.

Go through the gate and along the road towards the village, passing the Stonemason's Museum on the left. At the T-junction, with **The Cross Keys** pub ahead, turn right down **Brook Street**, passing the railway station on the left. Cross over the railway and canal to reach the car park on the right.

WALK 4

Fosbury Hill and the Chutes

Distance	13 miles (20.9km) or 10 miles (16.1km)
Time	6 hours or 4½ hours
Grade	3
Map	OS Explorer 131/Landrangers 174 and 185
Start/finish	Tidcombe church (SU291582); limited parking close to church
Public transport	None
Refreshments	Upper Chute – The Cross Keys Inn (01264 730295); Lower Chute – The Hatchet Inn (01264 730229); Vernham Dean – The George Inn (01264 737279)

This roller-coaster walk through the wooded downs on the Wiltshire–Hampshire border starts at the hamlet of Tidcombe and follows the delightful valley of Hippenscombe Bottom before climbing to pass through three of the Chute hamlets: Upper Chute, Lower Chute and Chute Cadley. The route then climbs again through the parkland of Conholt Park before descending to Vernham Dean, from where a final climb leads to the Iron Age hillfort at Fosbury. Then it's a fairly level walk over the downs before crossing the Chute Causeway and heading back to Tidcombe, with its charming manor house and Norman church.

Spend a few minutes looking round St Michael's Church in **Tidcombe**. The church mostly dates from the 14th century with a major restoration in 1882. There may have been an earlier church here, as the font is believed to be Saxon. From the churchyard there are good views of 18th-century red-brick Tidcombe Manor. The village was known as Titicome in the Domesday Book, derived from the Anglo-Saxon *cumb*, meaning 'valley', and *Titta*, a person's name.

This walk can be shortened by following the Chute Causeway shortly after Point 2, missing out the Chute hamlets.

① **SU291582** From the church walk up the road, bearing right at the junction and continue up the track. Close to the top turn left, following a track over the fields, to reach a road – **Chute Causeway**.

The **Chute Causeway** follows part of a former Roman road from Winchester (Venta Bulgarum) to Cunetio, now known as Mildenhall. Superstition claims that the road is haunted by the ghostly figure of a vicar of Chute. During the plague, the vicar is said to have persuaded his sick parishioners to go to a camp on the causeway, where they would be cared for. However, he never came back and left them to die. His plan failed anyway: he too died from the disease and was forced to wander along the road in penance for eternity.

Turn right for 300m and, at the start of the trees and scrub on the left, bear left along a bridleway beside **Scot's Poor Plantation**, keeping close to the fence. Continue straight on through a gate and follow the track along **Hippenscombe Bottom** to reach **Hippenscombe Farm**.

② **SU311561** Just past the farm turn right uphill along a bridleway – called Breach Lane – passing **Cleves Copse** on the left, to reach the **Chute Causeway** again.

Shorter walk

Turn left and follow the road to the junction – rejoin the route description halfway through Point 3 at SU322552.

To continue on the main route, cross over and continue along the bridleway (track). At the far corner of the small wood turn right, with trees to the left. Keep ahead, ignoring Breach Lane off to the left, cross over Drummer Lane and at the road turn left towards **Upper Chute**, ignoring the road to the right. Shortly after passing **St Nicholas' Church**, bear left at the junction and left again at the next; **The Cross Keys Inn** is about 400m off to the right.

Although there has been a church at **Upper Chute** since Norman times, St Nicholas' Church was entirely rebuilt in the 1860s. The oldest feature is the mid-Norman font (key available locally – details in the porch – if the church is locked).

Continue along Malthouse Lane, and 200m after the junction with Hookwood Lane turn half-right along a path between the fields, keeping ahead along the enclosed path, passing through some trees. Go left at the Y-junction, with gardens on the right, to cross a stile and turn left along the road. Bear right at **The Hatchet Inn** in **Lower Chute**.

The Chute hamlets lie in the hilly and relatively deserted border country between Wiltshire and Hampshire. The parishes of Chute and Chute Forest can be traced back to Norman times, and it is believed that the ancient meaning of Chute is 'wood' or 'forest'. Today there are five small hamlets: Upper and Lower Chute (both with pubs), Chute Standen, Chute Forest and Chute Cadley, which developed around what were once farms or country houses.

③ **SU311532** Continue along the road and bear left through the hamlet. Shortly after passing two lanes on the left and following the road slightly to the right, turn left along a lane passing the houses of **Chute Cadley**. Keep ahead along the track passing some woodland, cross a stile and then gently climb through the long field, keeping close to the left-hand boundary and Fisher's Hanger. Cross the stile and continue to climb through **Conholt Park**. At the top bear slightly right to reach a stile and road junction (**shorter walk rejoins here – SU322552**).

Once home to relatives of the Dukes of Wellington, **Conholt House** was more recently the home of Dutch tycoon Paul van Vlissingen. In 1977 he bought the remote and mountainous Letterewe Estate in Wester Ross; the access he granted to ramblers became a

The Hatchet Inn in Lower Chute

blueprint for subsequent national agreements on access to wild land.

Continue straight on in a northeasterly direction along the road for 450m and bear right at the junction for 50m. Turn half-left through a gate and along a path, keeping close to the right-hand field edge. Cross the stile and through the trees, following the path downhill and along the right-hand edge of Boats Copse to eventually reach the road in **Vernham Dean**; **The George Inn** is a short distance to the right.

④ **SU339505** Turn left along the road and, where it bends to the right, keep ahead over the stile and through the field to cross another stile. Bear slightly right across Conholt Hill road and follow the track between the houses to reach a gate. Continue uphill, keeping close to the fence on the right, and follow it round to the left. On reaching the gate at the top corner of the field, where a track comes up from **Warren Cottages** on the left, turn right for a few metres through the trees to cross a stile next to a gate. Follow the track up the right side of the field to the ramparts of **Fosbury Hillfort** (open access land), situated on the southwest end of **Haydown Hill**.

Fosbury Camp is a fine example of an oval bivallate (two concentric banks and ditches) Iron Age hillfort. There's not much to be seen on the tree-covered northern side, but the earthworks on the southwest side (overlooking the valley) are well pronounced, with a commanding view. Just inside the fort is a small dewpond, although the name is misleading: the pond is watertight and fills with rainwater run-off, not dew.

Follow the rampart round to the right to reach the area of conifers growing inside the fort. Turn right, cross a stile and follow a track through the earthworks before bearing left through Oakhill Wood to reach **Fosbury Farm**, with extensive views northeast towards Walbury Hill.

⑤ **SU314571** Continue west past the farm, ignoring the track (Tunball Lane) on the right, and after 500m go through a gate and straight over the cross-tracks; to the left is the combe, known as **The Slay**. Continue along the track, passing the track to Down Barn on the

The view from the ramparts of Fosbury hillfort

left, to reach a belt of trees. Keep ahead for 400m and cross over the road – **Chute Causeway**. Go through a gate and follow the path across the field next to the ancient ditch; on the left are the remains of a Neolithic long barrow. Continue downhill, staying close to the fence on the left, and at the fence corner head for the right-hand side of the small plantation at the bottom of the hill. Just after the trees, pass to the right of the small pond and follow the track up a slight rise and through a gate, then follow the road back to **Tidcombe**.

Haydown Hill looking west near The Slay

WALK 5
Faringdon's Folly

Distance	12 miles (19.3km) or 7 miles (11.3km)
Time	5 hours or 3¼ hours
Grade	2
Map	OS Explorer 170/Landrangers 163 and 174
Start/finish	Market Place, Faringdon (SU289956); long-stay car parking in Gloucester Street
Public transport	Bus links to Swindon and Oxford
Refreshments	Faringdon – selection of pubs, cafés and shops; Little Coxwell – Eagle Tavern (01367 240120); Littleworth – The Snooty Fox (01367 240549)

This circular walk starts in the picturesque town of Farindgon and heads over Badbury Hill, crowned with the earthworks of an Iron Age hillfort, before descending to Great Coxwell and the Great Barn, one of finest monastic barns in the country. The route then passes through Little Coxwell to reach the little village of Littleworth. From here it's an easy walk along a broad ridge back to Faringdon passing The Folly, which offers fantastic panoramic views south to the Lambourn Downs including White Horse Hill and north across the Thames Valley and Oxfordshire plain.

This route can be shortened by missing out Littleworth.

At the centre of **Faringdon** is the Market Place, its unusual 17th-century Town Hall surrounded by interesting old buildings including the Crown Hotel, a 16th-century coaching inn. Just to the north of the Market Place is All Saints Church dating mainly from the 12th and 13th centuries, with a fine Norman doorway and some interesting monuments. In 1864 the Faringdon Railway Company built a single-track railway line, laid to Brunel's unique 7ft gauge, from Uffington Junction to Faringdon. The line closed to all rail traffic in 1963.

① **SU289956** From the **Market Place** go along the A417 passing the **Red Lion**, and bear right along **Gloucester Street**. At the mini-roundabout go right (A417) and then left along **Canada Lane** and, where the road bends left, keep ahead along a track passing some houses. Just before the gate, turn right down through the trees to a kissing gate. Walk diagonally left across the field, keeping left of a large sycamore tree; continue along the left field edge. At the corner go through two kissing gates either side of a footbridge and take the left of two paths over the field to a kissing gate in the corner. Turn right and left to cross a footbridge and go through a kissing gate; continue diagonally across the field to a stile and gate. Turn left along a bridleway up through the field, with the hedge on the left to reach a gate. Continue up to pass another gate and keep ahead, passing **Badbury Hill House** on the right, to reach a gate.

Faringdon's
17th-century town hall

② **SU266947** Turn right down the lane and left at the wood along a path for Badbury Hill, firstly inside the wood and later inside the field close to the right-hand field edge. Cross a stile and continue through the wood to another stile, turn left up the path, later a track skirting round the earthworks of **Badbury Hill**.

Badbury Hill is the site of an Iron Age hillfort, probably dating from 600BC, and is crowned with a stand of beech trees, and a carpet of bluebells in the spring.

Continue through the car park and ahead along the road (left) for 200m; turn right at the footpath sign 'Great Coxwell Barn ½'. Follow the fenced track downhill and, about 20m before the bottom corner, turn half-left through the trees to a stile. Continue across the field and through a hedge gap to pass the **Great Barn**. Turn right along the road through **Great Coxwell** for 600m, keeping straight on at the junction, and later bear left to **St Giles Church**.

*The magnificent Great
Barn in Great Coxwell*

In 1204 King John granted the Manor of Faringdon to the Cistercian Abbey of Beaulieu in Hampshire, and by the mid-13th century the monks had built the **Great Barn**. This 150ft- (46m-) long tithe barn (a tithe was a form of income tax equating to one tenth of all agricultural produce) was described by William Morris (see Walk 1) as 'the finest piece of architecture in England, unapproachable in its dignity, as beautiful as a cathedral, yet with no ostentation of the builder's art'. The barn (now owned by the National Trust) remained under the control of Beaulieu until the Dissolution of the Monasteries in the 16th century.

The Church of St Giles in **Great Coxwell**, built around 1200, is dedicated to a hermit from the Dark Ages who is the patron saint of the disabled and homeless, and lies at the opposite end of the village. Each year the villagers celebrate the Feast of St Giles, gathering at the Great Barn to bless the spring from which the village probably takes its name – Cogges Well – before proceeding to the church for a service in honour of the saint.

③ **SU270934** Turn left in front of the church through the churchyard and a gap in the stone wall. Turn left and follow the edge of the field, before going right following a metalled path across the field and later passing the golf course to reach a road (A420). Cross over and take the disused road opposite; later bear left through **Little Coxwell**. Ignore the road to the left, but keep ahead to pass the **Eagle Tavern** on the left, later passing a path that leads to **St Mary's Church** (short detour).

> St Mary's Church at **Little Coxwell**, which at one time had links with the monks from Beaulieu Abbey, dates from the 12th century and has a few remaining Norman features.

Keep along the road and turn left at the junction along Fernham Road for 200m, then right following a gravel track (bridleway). Keep ahead to pass **Wicklesham Quarry** and farm, go over the disused railway bridge (Faringdon branch line) and follow the track (bridleway) slightly to left, keeping close to hedge. At the scrub ahead, bear left and follow the track downhill, later uphill to reach the A417 by some kennels (SU303951).

Shorter walk
Turn left along the A417 and carefully cross the A420 close to the roundabout. Walk round, keeping the roundabout on your right, and go through a gate into the field. Follow the field edge path for 100m and then diagonally left up across the field to reach a metal stile. Turn left uphill to reach a stand of trees encircling **The Folly**; admire the views. Take the metalled path in a westerly direction downhill for 400m, turn right along Stanford Road and left down London Street to the Market Place.

The view from Folly Hill at Faringdon

④ **SU303951** Turn right along the A417 passing the entrance to Charney Kennels, turn left at the entrance along the metalled drive (bridleway – 'Pusey 3½'). Continue past the farm, later Standford Place, and immediately after the Red House turn right in front of the gate to go through a small gate behind the garage. Follow the concrete track round to the left for a short distance and continue along the grassy track (unsigned) between the trees and fence, passing Oxpen Farm. Keep ahead through the field; go through a gap at the field corner and continue along the track. On reaching **Tagdown Barn** on the right, turn left between two open fields, later following the field edge round to the left, with a hedge on the right. Keep ahead along the grassy strip between the fields to join the A420; **The Snooty Fox** is to the right. Cross over and turn left along the pavement, passing the bus stop. At the junction go right down through **Littleworth** and follow the road round to the left.

⑤ **SU313971** Continue past the Victorian **Holy Ascension Church** and at the sharp right bend keep ahead along a gravel track, signed 'Church Walk to

Faringdon 1½'. At the garage ahead turn right and then left before the large gate to a stile and small gate. Follow the path over the field, cross a stile and bear half-left over the next field to cross another stile, just below **Haremoor Farm**. Keep ahead across a stile, with the fence on the left, to go through a gate, now with the fence on the right. Go through a gap in the field corner and turn left up past the house (Grove Lodge), following the driveway up to the road. Go left for a few metres and then right at the white metal stile, signed for 'The Folly'. Keep close to the trees on the right to eventually reach a white metal stile on the right. Turn right uphill to reach the stand of trees encircling **The Folly**; wander round the trees to admire the views, or go through the middle to see the folly.

The 100ft- (30m-) high **Faringdon Folly**, widely regarded to be the last tower folly built in Britain, was built in 1935 for Gerald Tyrwhitt-Wilson, 14th Lord Berners (1883–1950). Lord Berners, who lived at Faringdon House, was an accomplished writer, painter and composer. Stravinsky called him the best British composer of the 20th century and Diaghilev commissioned him to compose the score for the ballet 'Triumph of Neptune'. The folly, which is built of the site of a former medieval castle and Cromwellian battery, is open on the first Sunday of the month between 11am–5pm, April to October. From the top on a clear day there are said to be views over five counties.

Take the metalled path in a westerly direction downhill for 400m, turn right along Stanford Road and then left down London Street back to the **Market Place**.

WALK 6

Lambourn Downs: Striding out with Horses and Dragons

Distance	Day 1 – 11 miles (17.7km); Day 2 – 15 miles (24.1km)
Time	Day 1 – 5 hours; Day 2 – 6½ hours
Grade	3
Map	OS Explorers 158 and 170/Landranger 174
Start/finish	Market Place, Lambourn (SU325789); car park off High Street behind library, Lambourn (SU325788)
Public transport	Bus links to Newbury and Swindon
Refreshments	Youth hostel at The Court Hill Ridgeway Centre (0870 770 6064; **www.yha.org.uk**); camping allowed in the grounds
Refreshments	Lambourn – several pubs and shops; Eastbury – The Plough Inn (01488 71312); East Garston – Queen's Arms Hotel (01488 648757); Upper Lambourn – Malt Shovel (01488 73777)

Enjoy a magical weekend wandering over the Lambourn Downs, or opt for a long day walk. The route starts in the famous horse-training village of Lambourn and follows part of the Lambourn Valley Way (LVW), a 22-mile (35km) route between the Uffington White Horse and Newbury. All too soon, however, the valley is left behind in favour of the downs and the famous Ridgeway National Trail. The Ridgeway was designated as a long-distance route in 1972 and stretches for 85 miles (137km) from near Avebury in Wiltshire to Ivinghoe Beacon in Buckinghamshire. The trail follows the line of ancient tracks across southern England, many dating back more than 5000 years, making them some of the oldest roads in Britain. An overnight stop is made at the youth hostel at The Court Hill Ridgeway Centre, near Segsbury Castle. The village of Letcombe Regis, which has a pub, is just short of 2 miles (3.2km) away.

Day 2 continues along one of the most historically interesting parts of the Ridgeway. The high point of the walk is the beautiful stylised galloping figure of the Uffington White Horse and nearby Wayland's Smithy – two of the Ridgeway's most impressive sights. Thomas Hughes, author of *Tom Brown's Schooldays*, wrote of Uffington Hill as 'a place you won't ever forget' and how true that is – it is a special, even magical, spot. The route finally leaves this ancient highway behind, passing Ashdown House before reaching Lambourn.

The route can be modified into a rather long day walk of 18 miles (29km) by following the directions given between Eastbury (Point 2) and the Ridgeway.

Lambourn is situated in the Lambourn Valley, known as the 'Valley of the Racehorse' due to the large number of training stables in the area. St Michael's Church – the 'cathedral of the Downs' – has Norman origins, while

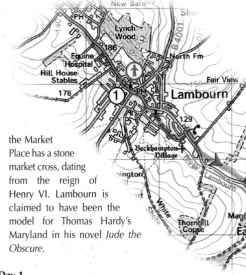

the Market Place has a stone market cross, dating from the reign of Henry VI. Lambourn is claimed to have been the model for Thomas Hardy's Maryland in his novel *Jude the Obscure*.

Day 1

① **SU325789** From the Market Place cross over the High Street beside the **George Hotel** and follow Newbury Street for 400m (the Lamb Inn can be seen ahead on the left), then take the path on the right, signposted for the **Lambourn Valley Way** (LVW). Continue between the buildings and across the playing fields,

keeping left of the clubhouse. Cross the stile and continue over the field to another stile.

Keep ahead along Bockhampton Road following it to the left over the **River Lambourn**, and
right at the T-junction along Newbury
Road heading away from Lambourn. At
the junction with Long Hedge
Lane

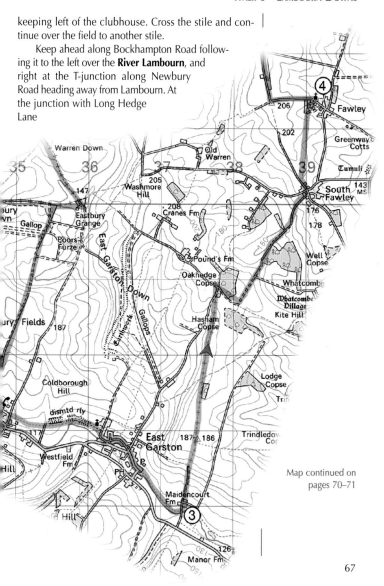

Map continued on
pages 70–71

take the path on the left (LVW), between the hedge and fence. Cross a stile and continue ahead through several fields following the LVW signs to reach a junction with a farm track just after passing a large barn on the left at **Eastbury**.

② **SU346774** Decision time!

One-day Walk

Turn left up the farm track heading out across the rolling downs. After about 1¾ miles (2.8km) turn right along the track to Grange Farm, and then left over **Warren Down** for just under 3 miles (4.8km), keeping straight on at the track junction to pass **Sheepdrove Farm**. Bear right along the road and at the junction turn left, following the Ridgeway. Now continue on the main (two-day) route from beyond Point 5, going west along the Ridgeway.

Two-day Walk

Turn right down the lane and left along the main road for a few metres – ahead is **The Plough Inn** – then right over the River Lambourn. Turn left along the lane running parallel with the main road, passing **St James the Greater** church.

> **Eastbury** is a small picturesque hamlet through which the River Lambourn flows. Although St James' Church looks old, it was built in the mid 1850s. The most interesting feature is the engraved window by Sir Laurence Whistler CBE (1912–2000), a fitting tribute to the poet Edward Thomas (1878–1917) and his wife, Helen, who originally lived at the village of Steep in Hampshire. After Thomas was killed in action in 1917 during World War I, his widow moved to Eastbury, where she remained until her death in 1967. You can see another of Whistler's windows at All Saints Church in Hannington (Walk 14).

At the junction, turn left, cross the main road and follow the lane uphill for 200m; turn right up the steps following the LVW again. Continue along the course of the disused **Lambourn Valley Railway** line towards **East**

Laurence Whistler's engraved window to the poet Edward Thomas in St James the Greater Church in Eastbury

Garston and, after passing the church go through the gate and along the fenced path. Turn right down the lane (Station Road) and then left through **East Garston**.

The 12-mile (19.3km) **Lambourn Valley Railway** opened in 1898, joining Lambourn with Newbury. The line merged with the GWR in 1905 and most of it closed to passengers in January 1960, but the section between Welford and Newbury operated until 1973.

The church passed in East Garston is **All Saints Church**, located close to Manor Farm. It is usually kept locked but it still has some Norman features, including the carved south doorway.

Continue ahead following the LVW along **Front Street**, and at the cross-junction keep straight on. Where the road bends to the right keep ahead along a farm track (LVW); the **Queens Arms** is a short distance to the right. At the left bend, leave the track and go across the field (LVW signs) following the **River Lambourn** towards **Maidencourt Farm**.

③ **SU373760** Leave the LVW and turn left up the track, passing through the farm; continue up the track, passing a trig point on the way. Follow

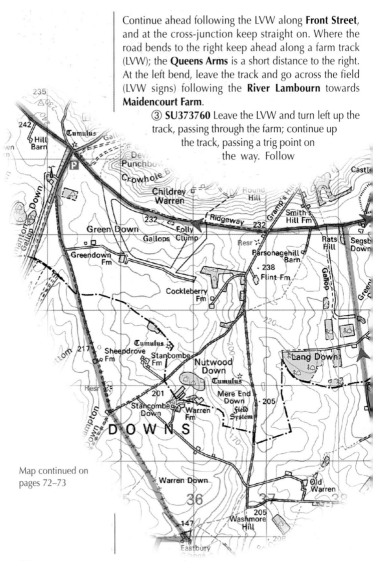

Map continued on pages 72–73

the track round the top edge of the trees at **Furze Border** and continue, following the fence on the left. Keep straight on at the cross-tracks and

later turn right along the lane. At the junction, beside Oakhedge Copse, turn right and, after 350m, turn left along a path over Kite Hill, following the track past Well Copse towards **South Fawley**. Go left along Dogkennel Lane and cross straight over the T-junction; continue for a short distance along the track and bear right on a footpath to **Fawley**. After crossing the open field, go through the gap in the trees, next to the footpath sign, and follow the fence on the left. At the corner go straight on – the path is very indistinct here – to reach the end of a garden. Follow the signs and turn right along the gravel drive.

Looking out over the famous White Horse on the Ridgeway

Fawley, known as Marygreen in Thomas Hardy's novel *Jude the Obscure*, was the setting for much of the story and 'Fawley' was Jude's surname. St Mary's Church dates from the 19th century and has some stained-glass windows by pre-Raphaelite artists Sir Edward Burne-Jones and William Morris.

④ **SU392813** At the road go left past **St Mary's Church**, and at the junction, next to the trig point, go right along

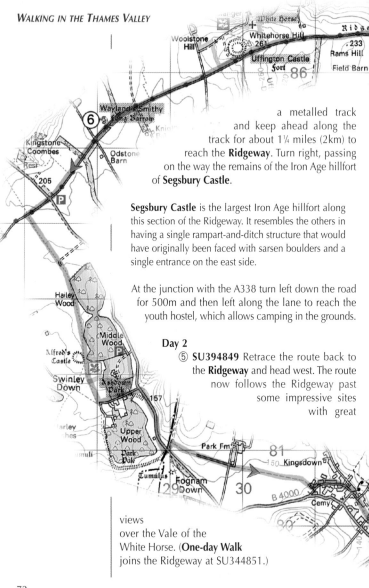

a metalled track and keep ahead along the track for about 1¼ miles (2km) to reach the **Ridgeway**. Turn right, passing on the way the remains of the Iron Age hillfort of **Segsbury Castle**.

Segsbury Castle is the largest Iron Age hillfort along this section of the Ridgeway. It resembles the others in having a single rampart-and-ditch structure that would have originally been faced with sarsen boulders and a single entrance on the east side.

At the junction with the A338 turn left down the road for 500m and then left along the lane to reach the youth hostel, which allows camping in the grounds.

Day 2

⑤ **SU394849** Retrace the route back to the **Ridgeway** and head west. The route now follows the Ridgeway past some impressive sites with great views over the Vale of the White Horse. (**One-day Walk** joins the Ridgeway at SU344851.)

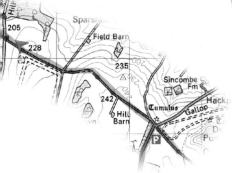

Detour

On reaching the top of **Whitehorse Hill** make a short detour to visit **Uffington Castle**. A short distance below is the famous **Uffington White Horse**. Further down is small, flat-topped **Dragon Hill**.

Whitehorse Hill, the highest point in Oxfordshire at 261m (856ft) is crowned by the remains of the Iron Age hillfort of **Uffington Castle**. From the ramparts there are fine views north over the Vale of the White Horse.

Uffington White Horse is the oldest such horse in the country and was first mentioned shortly after the Norman Conquest. Excavations in the 1990s dated the horse from around 1000BC, during the Bronze Age. The shape resembles engravings of horses found on coins minted by tribes who lived in this area in pre-Roman times, and may have been the symbol of the Celtic goddess of horses Epona, 'the great mare'.

G.K. Chesterton (1874–1936), in his 'Ballad of the White Horse', summed up the age of the horse perfectly:

> Before the gods that made the gods,
> had seen their sunrise pass,
> the White Horse of the White Horse
>   Vale,
> was cut out of the grass…

73

The figure's remarkable state of preservation has been put down to the 'scouring fairs' that used to be held every few years (the last major fair took place in 1857) where local people would gather to help clean it. Thomas Hughes, who spent his childhood in the village of Uffington, wrote about the area in *Tom Brown's Schooldays* in 1856, and also about the scouring rituals in the Victorian bestseller *The Scouring of the White Horse* in 1859. The small museum in Uffington, Hughes' birthplace (01367 820259) is worth a visit for those interested in his life and work.

The small, flat-topped, mound of **Dragon Hill** far below the White Horse is where St George is reputed to have killed the dragon. The bare patches of ground are said to have been caused by the dragon's blood, over which the grass never grows. The combe, to the left of Dragon Hill, is called The Manger, and legend has it that the White Horse goes there to feed.

Continue west along the Ridgeway and, shortly after crossing a metalled lane, stop-off at **Wayland's Smithy**.

Magical Wayland's Smithy

Wayland's Smithy, a Neolithic long barrow dating from 3700BC, is faced with large sarsen boulders at the

74

southern end. Excavations in 1962–3 found that it had been built on an existing oval barrow, which held the remains of 14 people in one large chamber. The second barrow, constructed some years later, contained the remains of eight people in two chambers. Wayland, a magical smith in Norse mythology, was first mentioned in AD955. Wayland was said to own a white horse and the close proximity of the Uffington White Horse may explain the name of this barrow. A local legend states that any traveller whose horse required a shoe should leave it with a coin next to the tomb; on returning the horse would be shod and the coin gone. The legend was referred to in Sir Walter Scott's novel *Kenilworth*:

> *You must tie your horse to that upright stone that has a ring in it and then you must whistle three times and lay down your money on that flat stone and then sit down among the bushes for ten min-utes. Then you will hear the hammer clink. Then say your prayers and you will find your money gone and your horse shod.*

⑥ **SU282853** Continue westwards along the Ridgeway, and shortly after crossing the B4000 take the track on the left through the field. Cross the stile and follow the path next to the right-hand field edge. At the fence corner continue straight on to reach a stile; to the right are the remains of **Alfred's Castle**.

Alfred's Castle is a small Iron Age hillfort or fortified farmstead, consisting of a single ditch and rampart with an entrance in the southeast corner. During excavation work pieces of pottery from the early Iron Age (500–300BC) and Belgic periods were found. The fort has been suggested as one of the possible mustering points for King Alfred's army in AD871, before defeating the Danes at the Battle of Ashdown.

Continue along the edge of the field; to the left is **Ashdown House**. Turn left past **Ashdown Farm**, and then right along the B4000 past the pumping station.

Ashdown House near the Ridgeway in winter

Ashdown House was commissioned by William, 1st Earl of Craven, in the 1660s and was described by the architectural historian Nikolaus Pevsner as 'the perfect doll's house'. The house was built for the love of Elizabeth of Bohemia, daughter of James I, who married Frederick V, Elector Palatine. In 1619 Frederick accepted the crown of Bohemia and Elizabeth became queen; however, they were driven into exile after just one winter and Elizabeth became known as the Winter Queen. Elizabeth died in 1662 without ever seeing the house. The four-storey building is constructed mainly from chalk, and has a massive oak staircase, hung with portraits of the Craven family. The house remained in the family until 1956 when it was given to the National Trust (for opening times call 01494 755569/01793 762209).

⑦ **SU290810** About 300m after the pumping station, turn left up a wide track and then right, following the bridleway for just over 1¼ miles (2km) to join a lane. Turn left and follow the high street through **Upper Lambourn** and at the junction keep straight with the stream on the left. Continue along the **Fulke Walwyn Way**. Take the lane ahead and at the junction, next to the **Malt Shovel**, follow the fenced path diagonally across the field and bear left along the B4000 towards **Lambourn**. At the junction with Big Lane on the left, leave the road and go straight on along **Threepost Lane**, passing **St Michael's Church** to reach the market place.

Walk 7

Thames Village Meander

Distance	12 miles (19.3km) or 10¼ miles (16.5km)
Time	5 hours or 4¼ hours
Grade	1
Map	OS Explorers 170 and 180/Landranger 164
Start/finish	Small car park in Orchard Road, Buckland, off A420 (SU345980)
Public transport	Bus links to Swindon and Oxford pass close to route
Refreshments	Buckland – Lamb Inn (01367 870484); Longworth – The Blue Boar (01865 820494); Newbridge – Maybush Inn (01865 300624); Rose Revived (01865 300221)

The walk starts at Buckland, sited on a low ridge between the valleys of the Rivers Thames and Ock – better known as the Vale of the White Horse – and follows country paths to the village of Hinton Waldrist, once part of a vast Norman estate. From here it's a short hop to Longworth before joining the River Thames at Newbridge, with a pub on either side of the river. Most of the return route follows the peaceful Thames Path through riverside meadow farmland, passing the Berks, Bucks & Oxon Wildlife Trust's (BBOWT) Chimney Meadows Nature Reserve before crossing over Tenfoot Bridge and heading back up to Buckland.

① **SU345980** From the car park turn right along **Orchard Road**, passing Wheelwright Court, down to the junction with **Summerside Road**. Turn left along a gravel track (footpath), later passing some cottages, and continue along the grassy track, passing a track to Rectory Farm. Keep ahead through the wood, and then follow the narrow enclosed path to reach a gravel track. Here either turn right along the track to the main road (unofficial route), or follow the path diagonally right across the scrubby area to the corner and join the main road (official route – but overgrown).

For a slightly shorter option, at Longworth miss out Newbridge and instead go over Harrowdown Hill to reach the Thames Path.

Turn left along the A420 for 200m, keeping to the verge on the left side, and turn left along the metalled drive (byway sign). Where this turns left, go straight on past the gate and through the wood; keep ahead along the track past **Great Pine Break** and go gently uphill to join a road. Turn left (straight on) towards **Hinton Waldrist**, and at the T-junction shortly after Manor Farm turn left along Church Road (signposted for Duxford) to a junction opposite the **Church of St Margaret of Antioch**.

During Norman times **Hinton Waldrist** was the centre of a large estate known as the Honour of St Valory; the St Valorys were cousins of William the Conqueror and built a castle here after 1066, close to the present church. Lady Mary de Bohun – daughter of the Earl of Hereford – lived in the village in the early years of her marriage to the Earl of Derby, who became King Henry IV; her son became King Henry V. The Church of St Margaret of Antioch dates from the 13th century, with heavy Victorian restoration.

② **SU376991** Turn right along the lane, and where it bends to the right (Prior's Lane) keep straight on along a bridleway – 'Longworth 1' – with trees on the left and a fence on the right. On reaching a stone wall ahead turn first right and left to follow the metalled lane past **Longworth Manor**. Continue past a small pond on the left and pass through the entrance gates; to the left is the **Church of St Mary the Virgin**.

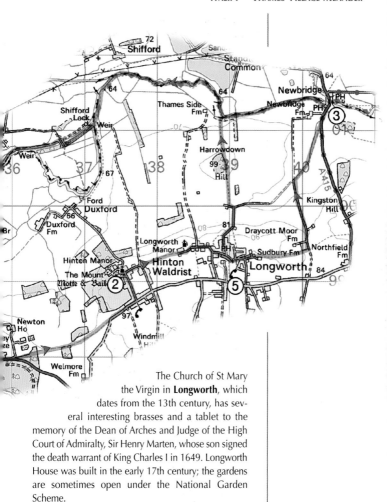

The Church of St Mary the Virgin in **Longworth**, which dates from the 13th century, has several interesting brasses and a tablet to the memory of the Dean of Arches and Judge of the High Court of Admiralty, Sir Henry Marten, whose son signed the death warrant of King Charles I in 1649. Longworth House was built in the early 17th century; the gardens are sometimes open under the National Garden Scheme.

Dr John Fell, born in the village in 1625, became Dean of Christ Church College, Vice-Chancellor of the University and Bishop of Oxford. Dr Fell was responsible for the building of the Tom Tower at Christ Church

College and the transferral of the mighty medieval bell known as Great Tom from the cathedral to the tower. However, he was an unpopular man and inspired the famous verse by one of his students, after a reprimand:

I do not love thee Doctor Fell
The reason why I cannot tell;
But this I know and know full well
I do not love thee Doctor Fell.

Two hundred years after Dr Fell the village saw the birth of Richard Doddridge Blackmore (1825–1900), author of *Lorna Doone*.

Continue along Church Lane through **Longworth** to reach The Square; a short distance along Tucks Lane on the left is **The Blue Boar** pub, which featured in the 1980s TV series *Private Schulz* and has an interesting collection of antique wooden skis dating back to the 1920s.

Shorter walk

Turn left along Tucks Lane past the **Blue Boar** and follow the lane downhill; at the track junction go left for a few metres and then right along a track sign-posted 'River Thames ¾ mile'. Follow the track over **Harrowdown Hill**, keeping ahead through the field with the hedge on the left. At the bottom left corner take the narrow path down through the scrubby trees to pass a small gate; continue ahead to the River Thames.

To continue on the main route keep ahead through the village, and where the road turns sharp right, becoming Cow Lane, keep straight on along Sudbury Lane for 120m. Where the lane turns left, go straight on through a gate just left of the entrance to **Sudbury Barn**; continue along the track, later between fields for 750m. At **Draycott Moor Farm** go between the pine trees, keeping to the right of the farm buildings, and turn left down the lane; keep ahead down the gravel track for 850m. At the junction ignore the track ahead but turn diagonally right, staying in the field, and follow the track along the left field edge. Bear left round the corner of the field and go through the gate; continue diagonally over the field to reach a gate a few metres left of the far right corner. Go through the trees, cross the footbridge and turn left along the road (A415) towards **Newbridge** (*care required*).

Newbridge claims to have the second oldest bridge on the Thames after Radcot Bridge (see Walk 1). It was probably built around 1250 by the Benedictine monks of Deerhurst Priory, near Gloucester, to which the manor of La Nore (Northmoor) – an outpost of the Abbey of St Denis, near Paris – belonged. The priory collected the toll money until 1460, when La Nore was seized from the French in the Hundred Years War. During the Civil War (in 1644) the bridge was captured by Oliver Cromwell, forcing Charles I to retreat north from his base in Oxford. The bridge has two pubs: the Maybush Inn on the south side and the Rose Revived on the north.

The River Thames at Newbridge – the second oldest bridge on the river

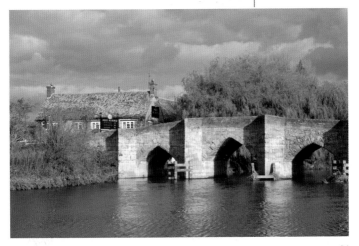

③ **SP404014** Just before the **Maybush Inn** turn left along path next to the inn, signposted 'Thames Path to Shifford Lock 2½'. Continue across the footbridge and through the gate; look back for a great view of the old bridge. The route now follows the **Thames Path** upstream for a few miles.

After about a mile, go through two gates either side of a footbridge (**shorter walk** rejoins here at SP389012), and continue along the Thames Path. At **Shifford Lock**, follow the Thames Path to the right over the footbridge. and with Shifford Lock weir ahead turn left through the trees passing a sign for **Chimney Meadows** (BBOWT Nature Reserve); the route is now following **Shifford Lock Cut**. Later cross the footbridge and turn left. keeping to the Thames Path along the right-hand riverbank to **Tenfoot Bridge**.

> **Chimney Meadows** is a 600-acre nature reserve cared for by the Berks, Bucks & Oxon Wildlife Trust since 2003, with the purpose of protecting important flood-plain meadows bordering the River Thames. Much of the area floods in winter, creating ideal habitat for curlew, snipe and other waders, along with many species of plants and butterflies.

> **Shifford Lock Cut** – the cutting through which the River Thames flows here – was created in 1897 to remove a shallow section of the original river, allowing boats to travel further upstream.

④ **SU354996** Cross the footbridge and keep ahead along the footpath to a junction with a bridleway; turn right along the grassy track for 550m, then left over the concrete bridge to follow a tree-lined track up to **Rectory Farm**. Turn right along the hedge-lined farm track gently uphill towards **Buckland**; later the track is metalled. At the top of the rise turn right along a grassy track and through a gate to walk through the churchyard of **St Mary the Virgin**.

The River Thames near Shifford Lock

The 12th-century Church of St Mary the Virgin in **Buckland** has a 19th-century clock by E.J. Dent, maker of Big Ben. There is a brass memorial to John Yate (d. 1578) and his wife Mary Justice, and also a monument to Sir Edward Yate (d. 1645) and his wife Katherine. The Yate family bought the Manor of Buckland in 1544 from Henry VIII. The house passed to the Throckmortons in 1690 when Mary Yate married Sir Robert Throckmorton.

Palladian-style Buckland Park (not open to the public) was described by Pevsner as 'the most splendid Georgian house in the county'. Built in 1757 for Sir Robert Throckmorton, the house was designed by John Wood, also responsible for the Royal Crescent in Bath.

Turn left along the path and leave via another gate; keep straight ahead along the lane. Go right for a short distance along St George's Road (continue further on for a view of **Buckland Park**) and then left along Buckland Road, before going left into Orchard Road; the lane on the right leads to the **Lamb Inn**. Follow the lane round to the left and then bear right back to the car park.

WALK 8

Hanging Around on Walbury Hill

Distance	12 miles (19.3km)
Time	5½ hours
Grade	3
Map	OS Explorers 158 and 131/Landranger 174
Start/finish	Car park at west side of Walbury Hill, south of Kintbury (SU370621)
Public transport	Limited bus links between Andover and Linkenholt
Refreshments	Faccombe – The Jack Russell Inn (01264 737315)

This circular route, which starts high up on the chalk ridge of the North Hampshire Downs, leads through three counties: Berkshire, Hampshire and Wiltshire. The walk heads west along the lofty ridge, with fantastic views across the downs, and passes Combe Gibbet. The ridge is left behind in favour of the remote hamlets of Buttermere, Linkenholt and Faccombe, tucked deeply beneath the downs. The final stage involves a stiff climb back to the ridge, before following part of the Wayfarer's Walk back to the car park. On the way the route passes over Pilot Hill, the highest point in Hampshire (286m/937ft) and Walbury Hill, the highest chalk hill in England at 297m (975ft).

This walk follows parts of the Test Way, a 44-mile (71km) route from Eling Wharf to Inkpen Beacon, and the Wayfarer's Walk, a 70-mile (113km) route from Emsworth on the south coast to Inkpen Beacon.

① **SU370621** From the car park walk west along the ridge up to **Combe Gibbet**. From here, on a clear day, there is a fantastic panoramic view: north over the Kennet Valley, west to the Wiltshire Downs, south across the Hampshire Downs and east to the Berkshire Downs.

Combe Gibbet stands on a Neolithic long barrow, dating from 3500–3000BC. The original gibbet was built in 1676 to hang local man George Broomham and his mistress Dorothy Newman for the murder of George's wife and son. Both were sentenced to be hung close to

Combe Gibbet

the site of their crime, their bodies left swinging as a deterrent to others; the gibbet was never again used for that purpose. The story of the murders was used as the basis of the 1948 film *The Black Legend*, directed by John Schlesinger.

Continue straight on along the ridge for about 2 miles (3.2km), and at the junction on Ham Hill (SU339618) go left along a track, Green Drove. On reaching the lane (Downs Lane) turn right past some houses and at **Town Farm** bear left towards **Buttermere**, passing Buttermere Pond on the left, to reach a staggered crossroads.

② **SU341610** Turn left at the junction next to the phone box, down Church Lane, passing the **Church of St James the Great**.

Situated at 255m (830ft) above sea level, **Buttermere** is the highest village in Wiltshire, with a church – St James the Great – reputed to be the county's smallest. The simple flint church still has its 13th-century windows.

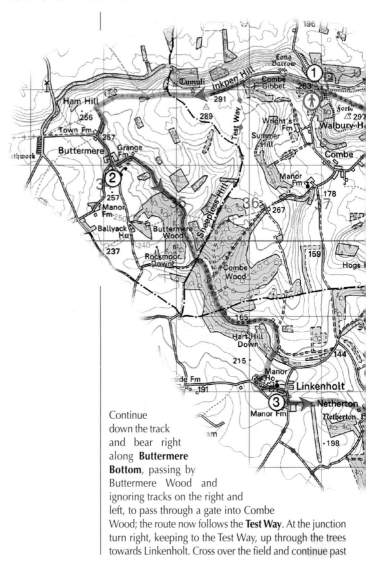

Continue down the track and bear right along **Buttermere Bottom**, passing by Buttermere Wood and ignoring tracks on the right and left, to pass through a gate into Combe Wood; the route now follows the **Test Way**. At the junction turn right, keeping to the Test Way, up through the trees towards Linkenholt. Cross over the field and continue past the manor house and bear right to join the road. Turn left along the road through **Linkenholt**, passing **St Peter's Church** with its picturesque wooden spire.

③ **SU365580** At the T-junction go right for 200m, then left along the signposted path, next to a large barn. Go through the gateway and follow the left-hand

field edge down to the bottom left corner. Cross over three stiles and continue through the trees and diagonally over the field. Cross a stile and follow the driveway down to the road in **Netherton**; turn right and then left at the junction, following the narrow road up towards **Faccombe** (*care required*). Bear to the right at the Y-junction to reach **The Jack Russell Inn** and turn left through the village, keeping to the right of **St Barnabas' Church**.

For many years the main village in the area was Netherton; however, within the last 200 years the population has drifted up to **Faccombe**. St Barnabas' Church, built in 1886, has a decorated Norman font and several 17th-century memorials from the original church in Netherton.

④ **SU390583** Just before the last house on the northern edge of the village turn right and follow the track (footpath sign) downhill, with **Roe Wood** on the right. Continue straight on at the junction to reach the valley bottom. The path now follows the track steeply up through the trees into open pasture. Keep to the left side of the wood near the top of the hill to reach the right-hand corner. Go left for 100m and then right over a stile; continue across the field to another stile and join the **Wayfarer's Walk**. Turn left along the track, passing **Pilot Hill** (286m/937ft) on the left; keep straight on at the road and at the small car park keep ahead, following the track through the earthworks of the Iron Age hillfort on **Walbury Hill** to reach the car park on the western side.

Walbury Hill is the highest chalk hill in England and is crowned by the largest Iron Age hillfort in Berkshire, covering 82 acres with a circumference of 1 mile (1.6km). The hillfort consists of a single rampart and ditch with two entrances. Walbury Hill, along with Inkpen Hill, forms the largest area of unimproved chalk downland in Berkshire, home to many types of chalk grassland flora. On the northern slopes, near the car park, stands a small plaque. This commemorates the fact that the area below was used in 1944 by the 9th Battalion, the Parachute Regiment in preparation for the successful assault on the German coastal artillery battery at Merville, France, before the invasion of Normandy.

The track over Walbury Hill

WALK 9
The Letcombe Gallop

Distance	12½ miles (20.1km)
Time	5½ hours
Grade	2
Map	OS Explorer 170/Landranger 174
Start/finish	Market Place, Wantage (SU398879); parking at Limborough Road off Mill Street (A417) (SU398881) or Portway off Church Street (SU397878)
Public transport	Thames Travel buses between Grove and Abingdon stop at Wantage
Refreshments	Wantage – pubs, cafés and shops; Childrey – The Hatchet Inn (01235 751213); Letcombe Regis – The Greyhound Inn (01235 771093)

The walk starts from Wantage and firstly follows the course of the old Wiltshire and Berkshire Canal (more commonly known as the Wilts & Berks Canal), opened in 1810 to connect the Kennet and Avon Canal with the River Thames at Abingdon. The route then passes Childrey before climbing the rippling downs, steeped in horse-racing tradition, to join the Ridgeway National Trail. After soaking up the views across the Vale of the White Horse, the route descends through the picture-postcard village of Letcombe Bassett and follows Letcombe Brook, once famed for its watercress beds, before passing through the village of Letcombe Regis to arrive back at Wantage.

The thriving market town of Wantage is famed as the birthplace of Alfred the Great in AD849.

In **Wantage** Market Place, which has some fine Georgian and Victorian buildings, is a statue of Alfred, King of the West Saxons, who defended his kingdom from the Danes before becoming overlord of England. Another famous inhabitant was the poet Sir John Betjeman, who lived here from 1951 to 1972. The much-restored church of St Peter and St Paul still displays many features from the original 13th-century

Alfred the Great's statue in Wantage

structure; the restoration was undertaken by well-known Victorian architect George Edmund (G.E.) Street, who lived in Wantage. Inside is a large 14th-century altar tomb to Sir William Fitzwaryn (d. 1361) and his wife Amica (the Fitzwaryns held the Manor of Wantage from 1207), and a superb brass figure of Sir Ivo Fitzwaryn (1343–1414), whose daughter Alice married Sir Richard (Dick) Whittington (1358–1423), three times Lord Mayor of London.

Opposite the church is the Vale and Downland Museum (01235 771447), dedicated to the geology, history and archaeology of Wantage and the Vale of the White Horse.

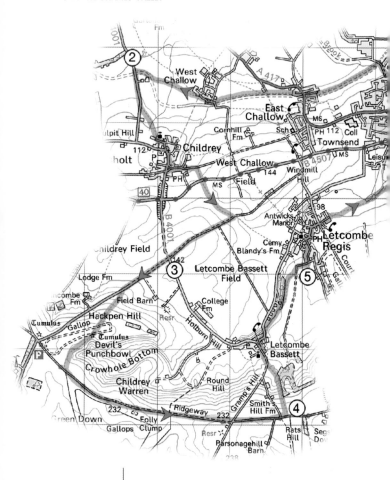

① **SU398879** From the **Market Place** walk west down Mill Street passing the **Bell Inn**, and just after Limborough Road (car park) turn right at the footpath sign. Keep to the left-hand path and cross over Denchworth Road, go north along St Mary's Way and then left into Wasborough Avenue to take a path to the right past **Stockham Farm**. At **Stockham Bridge** go left, following the course of the **Wiltshire and Berkshire Canal**, for just under 2 miles (3.2km), passing **East Challow** (detour to the left along the A417 for 100m to visit medieval **St Nicholas' Church**).

Completed in 1810, the 51-mile (82km) **Wiltshire and Berkshire Canal** was designed to connect with the Kennet and Avon Canal at Semington near Trowbridge and the Thames at Abingdon. The canal, which closed to through traffic in 1901 when a section of the Stanley Aqueduct between Chippenham and Calne collapsed, was completely abandoned in 1914.

On reaching **West Challow Bridge**, leave the canal and follow the road to the right towards **West Challow**.

The little stone-roofed St Laurence's Church in **West Challow** is claimed to have one of the oldest bells in England, inscribed 'Paul the potter made me' in Norman French, and probably cast around 1290.

Keep left at the junction, passing the village hall and **St Laurence's Church**. Where the road bends to the right, go straight on; ignore the bridleway off to the left, but take the left-hand path at the Y-junction across the fields and footbridge to rejoin the canal towpath and reach the B4001.

② **SU357887** Follow the road left for 400m, then left again at the stile and go along the signposted path diagonally across the field to the far corner, heading for **Childrey**. Go through the gate and continue straight on to a kissing gate leading through the churchyard, keeping to the right of **St Mary the Virgin Church**, to join Church Row.

> The north window in the Church of St Mary the Virgin in **Childrey** tells the story of the Virgin Mary's life, while outside the Cedar of Lebanon tree is claimed to be one of the oldest in Britain, planted in 1646 by the Rector, Dr Edward Pocock. Opposite the church is the early 16th-century manor house (remodelled in the 1900s), home of the Fettiplace family, local landowners during the Middle Ages.

Follow the lane round to the right and then along the High Street. Continue past the village pond, and just before **The Hatchet Inn**, take the metalled bridleway – Stowhill – on the left. After 400m turn right onto a footpath, cross the B4507 and continue along the path over the field. At the cross-tracks turn right up the byway – **Green Road**.

Looking east over the Devil's Punchbowl near the Ridgeway

③ **SU362862** Continue straight along the B4001 for 850m, and just before the telegraph wires turn left at the

steps up to the stile. Go diagonally uphill, aiming for the stile just visible at the top of the field. Cross two stiles and continue in the same direction across two more stiles to reach a stile to the right of the small tumulus. Go straight on to the next stile; the path now follows the fence on the right. To the left there are great views across the downs into the steep combe of the **Devil's Punchbowl**; cross the stile and follow the path over the field. Cross another stile and go left along the **Ridgeway** track, to eventually pass **Gramp's Hill** road and reach **Smith's Hill** road.

④ **SU377841** Continue for 100m past **Smith's Hill Road** and turn left at the stile signposted 'Letcombe Bassett 1', and follow the path steeply downhill. Go up a short rise, ignoring the path off to the right, to reach a stile at the fence. Cross over into the next field and follow the field boundary to reach **Gramp's Hill Road**. Turn right and follow the road down through **Letcombe Bassett**.

Thatched cottage in Letcombe Bassett, believed to be Arabella's cottage in Thomas Hardy's novel

Tucked beneath the downs, **Letcombe Bassett** has many picturesque thatched 17th-century cottages. In the Domesday Book it was known as Ledecumbe, meaning 'the brook [*lede*] in the valley'; the rest is derived from the Norman baron, Richard Bassett, who lived in the manor house in the mid-12th century. The mostly 13th-century Church of St Michael's and All Angels (partly rebuilt in 1861) has some fine examples of Norman ornamentation. To the left of the entrance is a blocked-up doorway, and still discernible are the four signs of the Evangelists: the Eagle of St John, the Lion of St Mark, the Angel of St Matthew and the Ox of St Luke. The church has six bells, the oldest dating from 1599.

Thomas Hardy used the village as the model for Cresscombe in *Jude the Obscure*; Wantage became Alfredston. The beautiful thatched cottage opposite the old inn, next to the stream, is said to have been the inspiration for Arabella's cottage, and is where Jude first met her. Jonathan Swift (1667–1745), Dean of St Patrick's Cathedral in Dublin, satirist, poet and author of *Gulliver's Travels*, stayed at the Old Rectory in 1714.

After passing Rectory Farm make a short detour along the lane on the left to visit the interesting **St Michael's Church**. Continue down Gramp's Hill and go right at the junction along the road signposted for Letcombe Regis and Wantage. At the junction with Rectory Lane, take the path on the right, to the left of the house and driveway, signposted for Letcombe Regis. ◀ Continue along the path eventually to join a track; go left and then right passing some houses to reach a junction.

⑤ **SU381861** Turn left down the metalled lane (South Street) through the village of **Letcombe Regis**.

'Regis' was added during the reign of Richard II, although **Letcombe** was already a Royal Manor to the Kings of Wessex, passing to William the Conqueror. Georgian Letcombe Manor is currently home to the Letcombe Agricultural Research Laboratory. Local

On the left is **Letcombe Brook**, once famed for its watercress which was sold as far away as London; some of the more recent cress bed structures still survive.

gossip has it that a previous owner, an Edwardian lady, was so shocked at two nude statues in the garden she ordered them to be sunk in the lake: during dredging in 1982 a 6ft- (2m-) high 2nd-century Roman marble figure of Hercules was found. St Andrew's Church, which dates from the 12th century, has the remains of a medieval cross just inside the gate.

At the crossroads, by **St Andrew's Church**, go right along Main Street towards **Wantage**, passing **The Greyhound Inn**. At the junction cross straight over Court Hill Road and along the lane (Manor Field); keep ahead following the signed path towards Wantage for about 1 mile (1.6km). Where the track splits, close to some allotments, take the left-hand fork. Cross straight over the B4507 (Portway), and continue along Priory Road. Bear right into Church Street and follow the road as it bears to the left round **St Peter and St Paul's** churchyard, before taking a narrow road on the right back to the **Market Place**.

WALK 10
Wantage and the Village Challenge

Distance	15½ miles (24.9km)
Time	6½ hours
Grade	2
Map	OS Explorer 170/Landranger 174
Start/finish:	Market Place, Wantage (SU398879); parking at Limborough Road off Mill Street (A417) (SU398881) or Portway off Church Street (SU397878)
Public transport	Thames Travel buses between Grove and Abingdon stop at Wantage
Refreshments	Wantage – pubs, cafés and shops; Letcombe Regis – The Greyhound Inn (01235 771093); East Hendred – Eyston Arms (01235 833320); The Wheatsheaf (01235 833229); The Plough Inn (01235 833213); Ardington – The Boar's Head (01235 833254); Smiths Tea Room and Bistro (01235 833237)

The walk starts out from the market town of Wantage, famed as the birthplace of Alfred the Great in 849. The route passes through the picturesque hamlets of Letcombe Regis and Letcombe Bassett, the latter immortalised as Cresscombe in Thomas Hardy's *Jude the Obscure*. A climb up to the lofty heights of the Ridgeway is rewarded with the earthworks of Segsbury Castle, an Iron Age hillfort. Before long the route descends to pass through East Hendred, awash with timber-framed and thatched cottages and a church that has an unusual feature – a faceless clock. When you reach Ardington, call in at the tea room for a well-deserved cream tea – Wantage is only a short walk away.

A long walk passing through several picturesque villages and following part of the Ridgeway.

① **SU398879** Head west from the **Market Place** towards **St Peter and St Paul's Church**, and turn left following the churchyard wall and bear right along Church Street (for information about Wantage see Walk 9). Go left along Priory Road and cross over the B4507 (Portway); follow a path ahead, and at the allotments go right then left, following the boundary. Cross the footbridge and continue along the path to join Manor Fields Lane in **Letcombe Regis**. Keep ahead and cross over Court Hill Road to follow Main Street past **The Greyhound Inn** and, at **St Andrew's Church**, bear left along South Street. At the T-junction turn right past some houses and, at the path junction, go left and bear right at the Y-junction to follow a path close to **Letcombe Brook**.

At the house go right down to the road and continue along Rectory Lane through **Letcombe Bassett**, bearing left up **Gramp's Hill** road (for more on Letcombe Regis and Letcombe Bassett see Walk 9). Just after the gentle right-hand bend, leave the road by going left through the gate and follow the field boundary on the right to cross a stile in the fence. Continue down to the hollow, ignoring a path off to the left, and then climb steeply, later crossing the field to reach the **Ridgeway**. Go left passing **Segsbury Castle**; the earthworks are accessible through the gate on the left.

> **Segsbury Castle** (Letcombe Castle) is a large Iron Age hillfort (2nd century BC). The design is similar to others along this section of the Ridgeway, a single rampart and ditch that would have been faced with sarsen boulders (see Appendix 2).

② **SU394844** At the junction with the A338, go right then left to continue along the Ridgeway. Shortly after passing **White House Farm**, follow the track left then right, and bear left at the fork in the track. Cross straight over the B4494 to continue along the Ridgeway; the **monument** on the right is to Robert Lloyd-Lindsay.

> **Colonel Robert Lloyd-Lindsay** (1832–1901), later Lord Wantage, was a famous soldier during the Crimean War, and was awarded the Victoria Cross. He was a founding member of the British Red Cross, and was also responsible for the statue of King Alfred in Wantage.

After about 2 miles (3.2km) turn left at the junction (SU445851), leaving the Ridgeway, and follow the bridleway down **East Ginge Down**. Turn right along the lane for a few metres and then left along a path next to **Ginge Brook**. At the cross-tracks go straight on; the path then bears right away from the stream to join a lane.

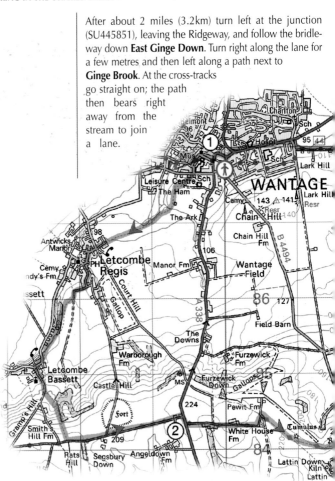

③ **SU446880** Go left towards **West Hendred**. On reaching a lane on the left to **Holy Trinity Church**, turn right over a stile and follow the footpath signposted for 'East Hendred ½'.

Edward I granted the manor of **West Hendred** to William Sparsholt in 1274. The 14th-century Holy Trinity Church houses a good Jacobean pulpit and some medieval glass.

Follow the fence on the right-hand side of the field to the stile in the far corner. Cross straight over the track and follow the bridleway for 750m towards **East Hendred**. Continue along the lane past the houses and at the junction continue along Horn Lane. Turn left down towards the village, passing **St Augustine's Church** on the left.

East Hendred, the larger of the two Hendred villages, has a wealth of 16th- and 17th-century brick and timber-framed houses. It was first mentioned in an Anglo-Saxon charter from 956 where it was called Hennerithe, 'rill of the waterhens'. After the Norman Conquest, the village was divided into five manors, including King's Manor and Abbey Manor, which were run under a feudal system. The church of St Augustine of Canterbury has a most interesting faceless clock, though this is hidden from view. Built in 1525 by John Seymour of Wantage, it is one of the oldest clocks in England, and still chimes the hours and quarters as it has for over 480 years.

The Victorian-Gothic Roman Catholic St Mary's Church, along St Mary's Road, was built by the Eyston family in the 1860s and has some good stained-glass windows.

St Augustine's Church in East Hendred

Hendred House, also known as the Manor of the Arches, is essentially an H-shaped 15th-century hall house. Originally owned by the Tubervilles in the mid-12th century, the house passed to the Eyston family in the 1440s with the marriage of Isabella Stowe (descended from the Arches family) to John Eyston, and has been their family home ever since. The family are related, by marriage, to Sir Thomas More, one-time chancellor to Henry VIII: the family still hold More's drinking cup and the staff of John Fisher, Bishop of Rochester (both executed on Tower Hill in 1535 for not renouncing the Catholic faith). The adjoining Saxon St Amand's Chapel was founded by Sir John de Turberville after receiving permission from Pope Alexander IV in 1256.

The village has two old customs: the distribution of flour to elderly people on Thomas' Eve (originally corn was given, which would have been ground into flour at the mill in Mill Lane), and on Shrove Tuesday when local children converge on Hendred House and sing 'Pit pat, pan's hot, Here we come a'shroving With a

The village shop – a fine example of early Tudor brickwork in East Hendred

103

batcher up my back A halfpenny is better than nothing.'
Each child is given a bun and a penny by Mr Eyston.

The little Chapel of Jesus of Bethlehem (Champs
Chapel) was built by the Carthusian monks of Sheen,
Surrey, in the 15th century. It's now home to the interesting village museum, which tells the story of this
once-thriving little market town (open Sunday afternoons in summer, first Sunday of the month in winter).

Continue along the High Street, passing the entrance to
Hendred House and then the village shop; the latter is a
fine example of early Tudor architecture. Further on pass
the **Eyston Arms** and bear left at the War Memorial and
Champs Chapel (museum), passing to the left of **The
Wheatsheaf**. Follow the road round to the right and then
left along Orchard Lane, passing **The Plough Inn**.

④ **SU458889** At the staggered crossroads go
straight on along Mill Lane, passing the **Hendreds
Sports Club** ground on the left. Immediately after the
next driveway turn left along a narrow signed path, following it round the back of the house and then along
the track. Where the track goes left through a gate continue straight on along the path with the fence on the
left. Go over the bridge and then across the field to cross
a footbridge. Turn half-left over the field to reach a stile;
follow the left boundary to the far corner. Cross the stile
and turn right along the track for a few metres, then left
at the gate following the left-hand field boundary. Once
at the corner, cross the stile to go along a narrow path
between the garden fences; continue ahead to reach the
road.

Turn right for about 50m and then left along a footpath signposted 'Ardington 1'. Follow the path, with the
fence and gardens on the left, across the field. After
300m go left for 20m and then right, following the fence
on the left. Continue past the field corner to reach a
small gate, cross the footbridge and turn half-left over the
field; keep to the track through the gap in the belt of
trees. Go across the fields aiming for **Ardington**, passing
some houses on the right to reach a road.

Ardington House

⑤ **SU435884** Go right through the village following the **High Street**; on the right is the village shop and Smiths Tea Room and Bistro (open 10am–4pm daily).

Detour
To visit **Holy Trinity Church**, **The Boar's Head** pub or **Ardington House** detour to the left down Well Street and left into Church Street.

Holy Trinity Church in **Ardington** (normally locked; the key can be obtained from the village shop) is situated close to the Boar's Head pub. The church dates from around 1200 and has a fine Norman doorway and a 14th-century churchyard cross, one of only a few in the county. Inside there is a marble figure by Edward Bailey, who also designed Nelson's Column in Trafalgar Square, and memorials to the Clarke family who have held the manor here for nearly 500 years.

The beautifully symmetrical grey and red-brick early Georgian **Ardington House**, home to the Baring family for several generations, was built for Edward Clarke in 1720, and once owned by Lord Wantage. The Barings – at one time wool merchants in Exeter – founded Barings Merchant Bank, which hit the world headlines when it was brought down by the unauthorised trading activities of Nick Leeson in the 1990s. The house – which has a stunning imperial staircase – is open during August and September (01235 833244).

Continue along School Road, and at the T-junction go straight on along the bridleway to join another lane; bear right, and at the sharp right-hand bend keep ahead along the narrow track. At the T-junction turn right along Lark Hill and then left, following the A417 along Charlton Road and Wallingford Street back to Wantage Market Place.

WALK 11

Farnborough: A Poet's Hideaway

Distance	12 miles (19.3km)
Time	5½ hours
Grade	2
Map	OS Explorer 170/Landranger 174
Start/finish	Bury Down car park, off A34 (SU479840)
Public transport	Buses between Newbury and Didcot stop at East Ilsley
Refreshments	East Ilsley – Swan Inn (01635 281238); Crown and Horns Inn (01635 281545); West Ilsley – Harrow Inn (01635 281260)

The walk starts high up on the Berkshire Downs to the south of Didcot and follows a section of the Ridgeway before descending to the village of East Ilsley, once famed for its sheep fairs. The route then continues over rolling countryside to the hamlet of Farnborough, where the poet John Betjeman lived for several years. From here it descends to West Ilsley, the original home of the Morland Brewery, before climbing back up to the Ridgeway and Bury Down.

① **SU479840** From Bury Down car park walk southeast along the **Ridgeway** for just under 1¾ miles (2.8km), passing under the A34, ignoring all tracks and paths off to left and right and passing a small memorial on the left. Finally turn right down a farm track (bridleway) at SU503825 with the gallops to the right – the second of the two tracks that are close together. Continue past the stables and along the metalled lane into **East Ilsley**.

A circular walk over the open downs where St John Betjeman and his wife loved to roam.

East Ilsley was once famed for its sheep fairs, second only to Smithfield Market, London. The market, which started during the reign of Henry III and continued until 1934, reached its peak in the 1880s when 20,000 sheep were changing hands in a single day. The village, which nestles round the duck pond, has several interesting buildings including East Ilsley Hall and Kennet House, two impressive early 18th-century houses. St Mary's Church was built in 11th century, though most of the present building dates from the 13th century.

② **SU495812** Turn right along Cow Lane and at the junction, next to the pond, turn left up Church Hill. At the lane on the right go through **St Mary's** churchyard, leaving by the steps over the west boundary wall, and bear right across the field to a kissing gate. Continue along the lane to join the High Street opposite Old Stanmore Road. Turn right down through the village and, at the **Crown and Horns Inn**, turn left along Fiddlers Lane, passing the **Swan Inn**. Follow the road under the A34 and straight on at the junction along a track (byway) – Woolvers Road.

Keep to the track on the left-hand side of the field, later hedged on both sides, passing **Windmill Down** on the left. Ignore the first two turnings to the right, but take the third, down a track on the right (SU474806). Follow this to the left, slowly climbing to pass the woodland of **Woolvers Borders** and reach a T-junction with Old Street on the western edge of the woodland. Turn right following the track, and after 150m go left down the track to reach the road near Catmore.

To visit **Catmore** and **St Margaret's Church**, turn left along the road for 150m to Catmore Farm. The simple church, which dates from the late 12th century, has been cared for by The Churches Conservation Trust since 1999. Adjacent to the church is Catmore House. This brick and timber house dates from the 14th century, although what you can see is mainly Elizabethan.

③ **SU454803**
Bear slightly right across the road and follow the bridleway uphill, with the wood on the left, and keep straight on at the junction with the byway. Where the track goes to the right round the edge of the field, keep ahead through a gap in the hedge. Continue across the field, firstly

following the slight depression and then bearing slightly left to reach the top of the field. At the Y-junction go left, following the footpath and keeping close to the field edge; pass through the hedge gap at the corner to cross a stile. Go diagonally across the field and then straight on to go through the next field, aiming for **All Saints Church** in the hamlet of **Farnborough**.

Farnborough sits high on the Berkshire Downs at 218m (735ft). The Poet Laureate Sir John Betjeman (1906–84), who loved walking on the downs, moved to the village with his wife in 1945. They lived at the Old Rectory, an 18th-century Dutch-style house, before moving to Wantage in 1951. The Old Rectory garden is open for a few days each year under the National Gardens Scheme (01488 638298 for information). Close by is the 12th-

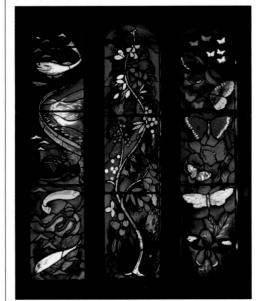

The John Betjeman window in All Saints Church in Farnborough

The Old Rectory in Farnborough

century All Saints Church, which underwent major restoration in the late 1880s. The colourful, stained-glass, west window was designed by John Piper in memory of his friend Sir John Betjeman.

④ **SU436819** After visiting the church go east along the lane, passing the **Old Rectory** on the left. At the corner, next to **Upper Farm**, go right (straight on) along a farm track – **Furze Lane** – and after passing a water tower leave the track and follow the path slightly off to the left over the field. Continue along the field edge and through the gap in the hedge to cross the next field. At the far side go through another gap in the hedge and turn left along the track – Old Street – for about 70m. At the sign, turn right (bridleway), following the fence on the left side of the field. Go through the gate and continue down the track, passing to the right of the farm buildings at Starveall Farm, to reach a road.

⑤ **SU462828** Turn right towards **West Ilsley**, passing the **Harrow Inn**, cricket ground and duck pond to continue along the Main Street.

> **West Ilsley** is often overshadowed by its better-known neighbour. On the west side of the village, the Harrow Inn overlooks the cricket ground and duck pond. Further along the Main Street is the old village school, rectory and church. All Saints Church underwent major alterations in the 1870s, though the underlying fabric is much older. The village was the original home of the Morland Brewery; John Morland, a local farmer, started brewing his much sought-after ale here in 1711, though the business moved to Abingdon in 1887.

At the junction, opposite **All Saints Church**, turn left up Bury Road (signposted to Chilton) for 150m and then right along a track, passing to the right of a large barn. Go through the small gate ahead and follow the narrow path up between the fences, before descending towards a thatched cottage. Follow the fenced path off to the left and keep ahead through the gate to follow the bridleway up **Folly Down**, passing through several fields and keeping close to the left-hand boundary fence. At the top of the hill go through a gate and turn left along the **Ridgeway** back to the car park.

WALK 12

Cold Ash and Hermitage: A Writer's Retreat

Distance	10½ miles (16.9km)
Time	4½ hours
Grade	1
Map	OS Explorer 158/Landranger 174
Start/finish	Village hall, Hermitage (SU505730); parking behind village hall
Public transport	Buses between Newbury and Didcot stop at Hermitage
Refreshments	Hermitage – Fox Inn (01635 201545);
	White Horse (01635 200325);
	Curridge – The Bunk Inn (01635 200400);
	Cold Ash – The Castle Inn (01635 863232);
	Spotted Dog (01635 862458)

The route starts at the village of Hermitage, once home to the well-known novelist D.H. Lawrence, and passes the tiny hamlet of Oare, before meandering southwards to the village of Cold Ash with some great views across the Kennet Valley to the North Hampshire Downs. The final leg of the walk passes through the villages of Ashmore Green and Curridge to arrive back at Hermitage.

Hermitage is a fairly busy village with a small white-washed church and a couple of pubs. Holy Trinity Church was built in 1835 by the vicar of Hampstead Norreys, personal chaplain to Queen Adelaide, wife of William IV. In 1882 the railway arrived when the line between Didcot and Newbury opened, followed by an extension to Southampton in 1885. Originally operated by the Didcot, Newbury and Southampton Railway (DN&SR), the line became part of the Great Western Railway in 1923 until its closure in the early 1960s.

The novelist and poet D.H. (David Herbert) Lawrence (1885–1930) and his German wife Frieda

A circular walk visiting several villages set in wooded countryside just south of the busy M4 motorway.

moved to Chapel Farm Cottage in 1917. Lawrence, author of such works as *Lady Chatterley's Lover*, spent two years at the cottage; the novel most closely linked with his time here was *The Fox*, published in 1923 and set at the fictional Bailey Farm, believed to have been based on Grimsbury Farm in Long Lane. The setting of the farm is recreated in the book, while the nearby market town is likely to have been Newbury.

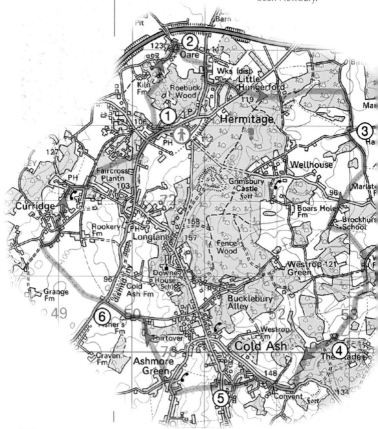

St Bartholomew's Church in Oare

① **SU505730** From the village hall in **Hermitage** turn right down **Newbury Road** and shortly turn right along **Doctor's Lane**. After 120m cross the stile on the right, next to the track junction, and head diagonally over the fields, crossing a stile and passing the power lines, aiming for the farm buildings. Before reaching the buildings, turn right over a stile in the fence on the right leading into woodland. Continue up through the trees, keeping left at the fork to follow the power lines for a time and keeping close to the fence on the left. At the track go left for 150m, passing a cottage on the left, and then bear right along a signposted path. Descend steeply through the woodland to a lane and keep to the right to reach Oare.

Oare, a tiny hamlet (which partly lost its air of tranquillity with the arrival of the nearby M4), has a history dating back to 968 when King Edgar gave 'Orha' to the powerful Abingdon Abbey. A priory, destroyed during the reign of King Henry VIII, once stood on the site of the present Oare Farm House. The delightful little St Bartholomew's Church, built in 1852 on the site of a previous chapel, was described by Sir John Betjeman as 'a Victorian gem set in the Berkshire countryside'.

② **SU506740** Just after **St Bartholomew's Church** turn right along a track at Oare Cottage, passing to the right of a pond. Cross the stile ahead and follow the left-hand hedge, cross the next stile and go right and left (now with the fence and a school on the right), cross another stile and turn right along the road. Turn left into **Chapel Lane**, following it over the disused railway, passing **Deacons Lane** and later **Pond Lane**. Chapel Farm Cottage – Lawrence's former home – is the first house on the left along Pond Lane. At the T-junction go left along Yattendon Road for 50m and then right at the footpath sign through the woodland for 500m to reach a broad track, and a sign explaining the open access policy to **Box Wood**. The Gerald Palmer Trust has granted open access for walkers to all the rides and paths within Box Wood. Follow the ride half-left and then bear to the right through the wood ◄ and at the far side, turn right along a track passing farm buildings to reach **Wellhouse Lane**.

③ **SU530729** Turn right for a short distance and then left along **Burntbrush Lane** (farm track). Shortly after a path on the left, go right at a stile next to the gate (overgrown), following a path diagonally over the field, and later following the left-hand field boundary. Cross straight over the road and take the lane down past the church at **Marlston** and **Brockhurst School**, both on your left, keeping to the right-hand fork at any junctions.

St Mary's Church in **Marlston** was built around 1270, though largely rebuilt in the 1800s. Two of its oldest features are the Norman north doorway and the church bell cast by Peter de Weston somewhere between 1336 and 1347; bells by this craftsman are rare, and this one is claimed to be the third oldest datable bell in Berkshire.

Note If the open access through Box Wood is removed follow the official right of way by going right along the broad track for about 100m and then left through the trees to cross a stile and follow the signed path over the field to the far side. Follow the path through Box Wood, and at the far side of the trees turn right along the track to Wellhouse Lane.

During renovation work in 1855 the exterior walls were faced with flint and the Annunciation window added. The Palmer family from the adjacent, rather grand, Marlston House (now Marlston and Brockhurst School), added the chancel in 1901.

St Mary's Church in Marlston

Just after passing the house on the left, turn left through the gate, with woodland ahead, to go through another gate and follow the path, keeping the field boundary on the left. After 250m fork diagonally right up across the field, passing the corner of the wood on the right, to reach a V-stile in the fence ahead near a large oak tree (SU531714). Continue up over the next field, passing to the right of some oak trees, cross the stile ahead and follow the path over the footbridge into the wood. At the far side turn right up the farm track passing **Withers Farm**. Where the track goes right, just after passing the gap in the hedge, keep straight on along the left-hand field edge. At the field corner go through the belt of trees and continue down through the next field. Turn right along the track – **Holly Lane** – through the trees.

④ **SU528702** At the road turn right past **Holly Farm** and shortly after the track (footpath) on the right, turn half-right along a signed bridleway down through the trees of **Holly Wood**. At the junction bear left along a footpath, follow it through the trees, and when you can see the small ponds in the field on the right climb up to the left through the trees to reach a road. Turn right towards **Cold Ash**, passing **St Finian's School** and **St Gabriel's Convent**. Turn left down the track (bridleway), and after a short distance bear right along the narrower wooded track. Cross straight over the road into Gladstone Lane and within a few metres turn left at the footpath sign along a track between the houses to reach another road. ◄

The **Castle Inn** and **Spotted Dog** pubs are both a short distance up the road to the right, with **St Mark's Church** a further 300m along Cold Ash Hill Road.

It was from around **Cold Ash** , during the Civil War, that Parliamentary troops launched an attack on Shaw House, forcing Charles I to abandon Newbury. The large red-brick St Gabriel's Convent was originally built as the private home of Lady Alice Fitzwilliam in 1912. She started a school for poor Roman Catholic girls here and in 1915 the ownership of the building was transferred to the Franciscan Missionaries of Mary, who continue to run the convent today.

Originally the hamlets of Cold Ash and Ashmore Green, together with several others, formed part of the extensive parish of Thatcham, and as such had no church until 1864 when St Mark's Church was built. The red-brick church stands at one of the highest points in the village and offers a commanding view.

⑤ **SU514696** Cross over the road and go along **Spring Lane**; later keep ahead along the fenced path to a stile. Cross over the track and V-stile to follow the left-hand field edge. At the top of the hill cross the stile next to the footpath sign and follow the narrow fenced path downhill; from here there are good views southwards across the Kennet Valley. Turn right along the road in **Ashmore**

Looking towards Cold Ash from near Ashmore Green

Green for 220m and then sharp left down **Stoney Lane** for about 150m. Turn right along the path following the left side of a small stream, between the houses. Pass through three small gates and bear half-left across the footbridge, then right for a few metres before heading left over the field, aiming for the footpath sign in the far fence. Turn right, keeping the fence on your left, cross the stile at the field corner and follow the path across the paddock to the buildings; continue along the concrete track to a gate. Go straight on along the drive past the house and turn left along Fisher's Lane (*care required – narrow road in places*).

⑥ **SU496697** At the T-junction keep ahead and take the track passing to the left of the house; keep to the left-hand fork (straight on) following the byway between the fields. Turn right at the junction and follow the track straight on past a house, and at the next junction turn left to reach **Curridge Road**. Go right for a short distance and then left along a narrow lane signposted for Curridge

Primary School; follow the lane round to the right in front of the school and then down the path. Turn left along the track (byway), passing several houses and ignoring a path to the left. Turn right at the T-junction, passing **The Bunk Inn**, and at the junction go left along the track – Crabtree Lane – for about 200m. At the footpath sign go diagonally right through **Faircross Plantation**, ignoring all other tracks and paths. After passing just to the right of a housing estate, go through the gap in the fence and keep straight on to reach the B4009. Turn left (pavement after the roundabout), passing the **White Horse** pub before arriving back at the village hall.

WALK 13

Blewbury and its Hillfort

Distance	13 miles (20.9km)
Time	5½ hours
Grade	1
Map	OS Explorer 170/Landranger 174
Start/finish	Cholsey railway station (SU584861); parking (pay and display) at station car park; alternative start at St Mary's Church (SU584870)
Public transport	Trains to Cholsey from Paddington and Oxford, bus links to Wallingford
Refreshments	South Moreton – The Crown (01235 812262); East Hagbourne – Fleur de Lys (01235 813247); West Hagbourne – Horse and Harrow (01235 850223); Upton – George & Dragon (01235 850723); Blewbury – Load of Mischief (01235 851076); Red Lion (01235 850403); Barley Mow (01235 850296); Aston Tirrold – Chequers Inn (01235 851272)

A fairly level walk on the northern edge of the Berkshire Downs that passes through several peaceful villages in south Oxfordshire, with plenty of thatched cottages, old pubs and interesting churches. The route starts in the village of Cholsey – resting place of famous crime writer Agatha Christie – and passes through the picturesque villages of East and West Hagbourne, separated by the Great Fire of Hagbourne in 1659. It then heads for Blewbury, overlooked by the remains of an Iron Age hillfort on Blewburton Hill, before passing through the twin villages of Aston Upthorpe and Aston Tirrold back to Cholsey.

① **SU584861** From the railway station go down to the crossroads and turn left. Continue along the road as it bears to the right, and at its junction with **Sandy Lane** go left along a signed footpath between the fences. At the stream go left, ignoring the footbridge on the right, to pass

This walk can also be started and finished from St Mary's Church in Cholsey.

under the railway line. Immediately turn right to cross a
footbridge and go through the kissing gate; continue over
the field keeping the branch line – **Cholsey and
Wallingford Railway** – on the right, going away from the
main railway line.

Cholsey and Wallingford Railway A preserved former
Great Western Railway branch line built in 1863.
Known locally as 'The Bunk', the line closed to pas-
senger services in 1959, though it continued to serve
the malt plant in Wallingford until 1981, at which time
the preservation society was formed. Trains, some

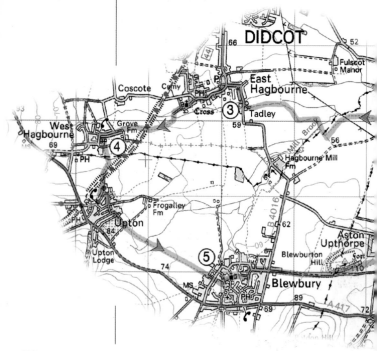

steam-driven, operate at certain times throughout the
year (01491 833067).

Cross another footbridge, then through a gate to go diagonally over the field, heading for a gate in the churchyard wall. Follow the path through **St Mary's** churchyard
and turn right in front of the church to reach the car park
(*alternative start point*).

Cholsey St Mary's Church was founded over 1000 years
ago, though was substantially rebuilt in the 12th century
and later restored by the Victorians. The famous crime
writer Agatha Christie (1890–1976), who lived at
Winterbrook House, is buried alongside her husband,
archaeologist Sir Max
Mallowan, in the
northwest cor-
ner of the

churchyard. Christie (real name Agatha Mary Clarissa Mallowan, née Miller) is best known as the creator of Miss Marple and Hercule Poirot and for her thriller *The Mousetrap*, the world's longest-running play, which opened in November 1952.

Turn left along the road, passing **Manor Farm**, and where the road bends to the left go right along a signposted path diagonally across the field, aiming for Wittenham Clumps (which can be seen in the distance). At the brow of the field, turn half-left along a path following the old boundary line between two fields. Cross the road and stile, keeping the hedge on the right, and at the field corner cross the footbridge and turn left, then bear right through the trees into another field. Follow the right-hand field boundary, with the stream on the right. Eventually cross over at the footbridge and turn left, keeping close to the stream. Turn right at the field corner, then left through a short tunnel under the main railway line. Turn half-right along a fenced path for 150m and at the junction go left along the hedged path. Continue along Crown Lane, passing **The Crown** in **South Moreton** on the left.

South Moreton's name is derived from the Saxon Moretun or 'town on the moor'. The parish church, dedicated to St John the Baptist, is mostly 13th and 14th centuries, though there are remains of a Saxon west door. The irregular circular mound next to the church is thought to be the remains of a Norman Conquest castle. To the north of The Crown is the old manor house (Sanderville Manor), with the remains of a moat built during the reign of King Stephen in the 1150s. The railway line just to the north of the village is the Great Western Railway from London heading for Didcot and the Westcountry, built by the renowned engineer Isambard Kingdom Brunel in the 1850s.

② **SU561882** Turn right along the **High Street** for about 200m, passing the **Strict Baptist Chapel** on the right (founded in 1832), and then left along **Church Lane**. At

Timber-framed cottage in East Hagbourne

the **St John the Baptist Church** turn left along a fenced path and then right, following a path next to the wall on the left. Cross the footbridge and immediately turn right across another footbridge and stile. Go through the field, keeping the stream on the right, cross a footbridge, and turn left over a stile and then right. Cross the footbridge and stile to go through the narrow field, cross another stile and go through the field, with the boundary and stream on the right. At the corner bear left to follow the next field edge, continue under the power lines and pass to the right of an oak tree. At the field corner go left for a short distance and then right through the gap in the hedge; turn right over the field and cross the footbridge over **Mill Brook**, a few metres to the left of the field corner. Continue along the bridleway, keeping close to the field boundary on the right, eventually to reach **Blewbury Road** (B4016) in **East Hagbourne**.

The earliest mention of a village at **East and West Hagbourne** was in a charter of King Alfred's where it was known as Haccaburna. Despite its proximity to Didcot, East Hagbourne remains very picturesque, with many thatched and timber-framed cottages. Along the Main Road is the Upper Cross, a large medieval cross with three sundials. Norman St Andrew's Church has several interesting features, including its 600-year-old north door.

Originally East and West Hagbourne were joined, but in 1659 the Great Fire of Hagbourne destroyed the cottages between the church and West Hagbourne. After the fire, Charles II appealed to the people of London to collect money for the villagers; in 1666 the Great Fire of London inspired the people of Hagbourne to return their charity. West Hagbourne has a cluster of houses round a small village green and duck pond.

③ **SU533882** Turn right along the road and left at the junction, next to the war memorial and stump of an old medieval cross, **Lower Cross**. Follow the raised pathway, passing the **Fleur de Lys** pub, to reach **Upper Cross** (medieval cross). Keep ahead along Church Close and go through the churchyard, passing **St Andrew's Church**. Cross the V-stile and keep ahead next to the brick wall, later along a metalled path. Cross the stream and turn right to pass under the disused railway embankment, following the track to **West Hagbourne**.

④ **SU515878** Go straight on along **Foxglove Lane** and left at the junction, passing the village pond. Continue along the gravel track for a short distance and, just before Manor Farm, turn left. At the Y-junction, just past the farmyard, follow the right-hand path and cross the bridge and stile. Continue across the field to the far corner, cross the stile next to the gate and go under the disused railway embankment. Follow the track towards **Upton**, and go left at the junction for a short distance, then right along Church Street, passing **St Mary's Church**; keep ahead at the crossroads.

St Michael's Church in Blewbury

Famed for its apple and damson orchards during the 19th century, **Upton** at one time paid tithes to the Cluniac priory of Bermondsey. St Mary's Church was built between the 11th and 12th centuries on the site of an earlier structure, and restoration work carried out in 1885. The nearby disused railway line was the Didcot, Newbury and Southampton Railway (DN&SR), which operated between 1882 and 1962; the local station was at Upton.

Where the road goes to the right, turn left along the track, and bear right along the path signposted 'Footpath Blewbury 1'. Go straight on, with the orchard on the right, and then over the open fields, crossing a stream on the way. After passing the telegraph pole follow the path between the buildings to reach Westerbrook Street in **Blewbury**.

Once home to Kenneth Grahame (1859–1932), Secretary to the Bank of England – though better known as author of *The Wind in the Willows* – **Blewbury** has many timbered buildings and thatched roofs, and some original thatched cob boundary walls. The village was first mentioned as Bloebyrig in a Saxon charter from King Edmund in 944, although by the time of the Domesday Book – by then quite large with a church and four mills – it was known as Blitberie. St Michael's Church has Saxon origins, though rebuilt in the 11th century. Inside are some interesting memorial brasses, including one to Dame Alice Daunce (d. 1523) and her husband Sir John, Surveyor-General to Henry VIII.

⑤ **SU529859** Cross slightly to the left and keep ahead along Curtoys Lane, at the cross-junction – The Red Lion is a short distance off to the right – go left to pass **St Michael's Church**. Turn right along Church End, passing the Rectory, and keep ahead along a narrow footpath, next to the stream, leading to Watt's Lane. At the T-junction turn left down South Street for 150m ◄ and then

The Load of Mischief pub is to the right along South Street, with The Barley Mow at the junction with the A417.

Earthworks of Blewburton hillfort

right along Bessels Lea road to reach **Bessel's Way** (B4016). Cross straight over and follow the farm track 'Bridleway Aston Upthorpe 1', passing **Winterbrook Farm**, with views towards Blewburton hillfort ahead. Continue along the southern side of Blewburton Hill; detour through the gate on the left to visit the top of **Blewburton Hill** (open access land).

> **Blewburton Hillfort** was originally built as a palisaded settlement, one of the earliest types of defensive barrier used on hillforts, though it was later refortified. The fort was abandoned during the Romano-British period, before being used as a cemetery by the Anglo-Saxons.

Bear left at the stile (SU547860) along a path following the outline of the hill before descending some steps. Continue along the lane, following it first left and then right past **All Saints Church** in **Aston Upthorpe**. Turn right along Spring Lane for 150m and then left next to the United Reform Church. Continue straight over the junction with Baker Street and later Rectory Lane to pass **St Michael's Church** in **Aston Tirrold**. Turn right along Aston Street for 400m.

The twin villages of **Aston Tirrold** and **Aston Upthorpe** at the foot of the Berkshire Downs have a Presbyterian tradition, and 'meetings in the barns' were fairly common before the Act of Uniformity in 1662. The interesting Presbyterian Chapel, now the United Reform Church, was built in 1728, making it one of the oldest in England. Aston Upthorpe's All Saints Church is built on Saxon foundations and has an 11th-century nave and filled Norman doorway. St Michael's Church, in Aston Tirrold, dates back to 1080.

⑥ **SU556857** Shortly after the junction of **Aston Street** and **Baker Street**, go left along a track (bridleway to Cholsey) with a big house on the left and the playing field on the right. Now follow the bridleway ahead to pass **Lollingdon Farm**; where the lane bears to the right go straight on into the field, following the hedge on the left.

At Westfield Farm keep ahead along a fenced path, passing under the power lines, to reach a road just to the right of a house. Turn right for a few metres and then left along a lane, later a gravel track to pass under the railway line. Turn right along the road and right again at the crossroads to reach the railway station.

Alternative start/finish
From the railway station follow directions under Point 1 to reach St Mary's Church.

WALK 14

Watership Down: A Land of Rabbits

Distance	14¼ miles (22.9km) or 8½ miles (13.7km)
Time	6½ hours or 4 hours
Grade	3
Map	OS Explorer 144/Landranger 174
Start/finish	Car park in Anchor Road, off Swan Street, Kingsclere (SU527586)
Public transport	Buses between Newbury and Basingstoke stop at Kingsclere
Refreshments	Kingsclere – The Crown (01635 299558); The Swan Hotel (01635 298314); The George and Horn (01635 298649); village shop; Hannington – The Vine (01635 298525)

Follow this roller-coaster figure-of-eight route over the rolling chalk hills of the North Hampshire Downs to the south of Newbury, an area immortalised in Richard Adams' book *Watership Down*. The walk starts at the village of Kingsclere – one of the three 'clere' villages and famed for its horse-racing stables – before climbing up towards Watership Down with its far-reaching views. The route continues to Ladle Hill before descending to Sydmonton Court, then heads back up to the ridge and follows part of the Wayfarer's Walk – a long-distance route between Emsworth and Inkpen Beacon – to reach Hannington. From here it's a gentle descent back to Kingsclere.

Kingsclere is the largest of the 'clere' villages (with Burghclere and Highclere). Once a royal manor, the area is famed for its horse-racing stables, which have produced several Derby winners over the years; the soft, springy turf of the downs provides the perfect training ground. St Mary's Church, extensively restored in 1848, has Norman origins and is worth a visit with its Norman north doorway, 14th-century

For a shorter walk, the loop that takes in both Ladle Hill and Sydmonton Court can be easily missed out at Point 2.

Kingsmill Chapel and many medieval floor tiles. The tower has a bed-bug weather vane: legend has it that it was given by King John, who suffered from them while staying at a local inn.

① **SU527586** From the car park head down **Anchor Road** and across **Swan Street** into **St Mary's** church-yard. Follow the path left of the church, next to the building on the left, and bear left at the hedge, leaving the churchyard along a narrow enclosed path. Continue over two footbridges and follow the path left and right to reach Fox's Lane. Turn left and at the junction bear right; after 400m turn left at a footpath sign through the gate in the hedge.

Head southwest, keeping the gallop on your right; **Watership Down** is straight ahead. After about 600m turn left at a post with a yellow arrow and walk over the field for 500m to a T-junction.

Turn right along the track for 600m to reach another post with a yellow arrow pointing off to the left, just before the field boundary. Walk up through the trees, cross the stile and continue diagonally uphill. At the fence turn right and follow it to a stile, 10m right of the field corner. Follow the path diagonally to the left, cross over the cinder gallop and continue to a gate (SU500569) in the fence.

Shorter walk

Turn left at the gate and follow the track to cross over the B3051 and rejoin the main route at Point 4.

② **SU500569** From the gate turn right and follow the track – **Wayfarer's Walk** – west to the top of **Watership Down** with its extensive views across the Kennet Valley.

The tree-lined track from Ladle Hill towards Watership Down

Watership Down is situated on a delightful chalk ridge that stretches for 10 miles (16km) from the Wiltshire border, forming part of the North Hampshire Downs. The area has enjoyed almost legendary status since the author Richard Adams, born in Newbury, chose it as the setting for his best-selling story *Watership Down*, based on the adventures of a group of rabbits.

Cross the stile and follow the fence downhill, cross over the lane and continue along the track for 300m to go through a gate on the right. Follow the track uphill, keeping close to the fence, and continue over the top of the hill. At the gate in the hedge ahead turn left for 150m and then right to reach **Ladle Hill**. To the right, through the gate, are the remains of an Iron Age hillfort; looking west you can see **Beacon Hill**, crowned with another.

Beacon Hill is the resting place of George Edward Stanhope Molyneux Herbert – 5th Earl of Carnarvon (1866–1923) – who funded the expedition that discovered the tomb of Tutankhamen in the Valley of the Kings, Egypt, in 1922. The earl died shortly after in Cairo, which some put down to the Curse of Tutankhamen. Beacon Hill overlooks Highclere Castle, home to the Earls of Carnarvon.

Continue close to the fence for 150m, then go left across the open field. Just before a stand of trees and scrub, turn sharp right over the field to reach a gate, descend through the scrub and along the tree-lined track to the road.

③ **SU478580** Keep ahead following the road, signposted to 'Burghclere 2', and just after **Wergs Farm** turn right along a track past two houses. At the end of the trees turn sharp right, cross a stile, and follow the road through **Sydmonton Court**.

The **Sydmonton Court** estate, named after Sydeman who was mentioned in AD931 and the Old English *tun* meaning 'farm', was owned by Romsey Abbey until the Dissolution of the Monasteries in the 16th century. The estate was then granted to William Kingsmill, and stayed in the family line for many generations. Sydmonton Court is now the country home of Lord Lloyd Webber of Sydmonton (better known as Andrew Lloyd Webber). Visible in the trees on the left is St Mary's Church (private), built in the 1850s though appearing much older.

At the red postbox go straight on along the grass between the hedge and wall to a stile. Turn left along the road for 200m, then right at the footpath sign and stile. Follow the track to **Barton Copse**, cross a stile and bear left uphill. After passing a large pylon go through the small gate and turn left along the track – **Wayfarer's Walk**. Cross the lane and retrace the route back up over **Watership Down** to the gate at SU500569 (**shorter**

walk rejoins here). From the gate, continue along the track for 1 mile (1.6km), and cross over the road (B3051).

④ **SU516565** Take the narrow hedged path to the right of the car park entrance and continue along the **Wayfarer's Walk**, signposted 'Emsworth 53½ miles'. Keep to the right-hand field boundary up the hill, and then along the enclosed path. Turn left along the lane for a few metres, and just after the entrance for **Walkeridge Farm** turn right through the gate and follow the field boundary off to the left along two sides of the field. Turn left through the gate in the hedge and continue following the field boundary on the right. On reaching the large barn, take the footpath through the small gate, passing to the right of the barn. At **Manor Farm** follow the enclosed path to the left of the buildings, before going right round an old barn. Turn left along the gravel drive, with **All Saints Church** on the right, and continue past the village green and wellhead (built in 1897 to celebrate Queen Victoria's jubilee) to reach the main road in **Hannington**.

> All Saints Church, next to the village green in **Hannington**, dates back to Saxon times, with additions in the 12th and 19th centuries. There are two modern memorial windows designed and engraved by Sir Laurence Whistler CBE (1912–2000), a leading exponent of hand engraving during the 20th century. You can see another of his windows at St James' Church in Eastbury (see Walk 6).

⑤ **SU539555** The route continues to the left along the road. ◀ At the T-junction go left along **Meadham Lane**, and after passing the last property on the right turn right through a metal gate and go along the track (bridleway). After crossing under the power lines follow the track first left, then right past Hannington Scrubs, down into the hollow and up the other side. Keep ahead at the cross-tracks and follow the track downhill, with **Cottington's Hill** and the wooded slope of **Freemantle**

A short distance to the right is **The Vine** pub.

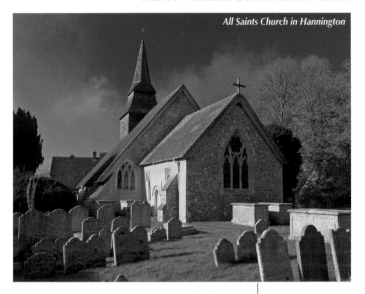

All Saints Church in Hannington

Park Down to the left. ▶ Continue north over the field for 700m to join a farm track, turn left for a few metres to a junction and then take the left-hand tree-lined track – **Hollowshot Lane**. Just before the first property on the left, turn right at a stile, follow the path and steps between the paddocks to enter the playing field by a kissing gate. Follow the left-hand side to leave at the bottom corner and shortly turn right down a path leading to a road and back to the car park.

This area was a royal hunting forest used by King John and his son Henry III in the early 1200s.

WALK 15

The Pang Valley: A River Runs Through It

Distance	12½ miles (20.1km) or 8½ miles (13.7km)
Time	5¼ hours or 3¾ hours
Grade	1
Map	OS Explorer 159/Landranger 174
Start/finish	Bladebone Inn at Chapel Row (SU571697): small parking area on edge of common close to inn (SU571697)
Public transport	Buses between Newbury and Reading stop at Bucklebury–Bladebone
Refreshments	Chapel Row – Bladebone Inn (0118 971 2326), village shop and tea room; Frilsham – Pot Kiln (01635 201366); Stanford Dingley – The Bull (0118 974 4582); The Old Boot (0118 974 4292)

This circular route meanders its way through the picturesque Pang Valley in Berkshire, where the River Pang – which rises in the Berkshire Downs beyond Hampstead Norreys – flows gently towards the River Thames at Pangbourne. The walk starts at Chapel Row and passes over Bucklebury Common, a staging post for Oliver Cromwell's army on their way to the Second Battle of Newbury during the Civil War in 1644, before descending to the peaceful village of Bucklebury and continuing towards Frilsham. From Stanford Dingley the route follows the course of the River Pang to Bradfield, famed for its school. The final stretch wanders through a patchwork of woodland passing the little hamlets of Rotten Row, Tutts Clump and Jennetts Hill before arriving back at Chapel Row with its pub and village tea room.

The walk can be shortened by missing out the Stanford Dingley–Bradfield section.

① **SU571697** From the **Bladebone Inn** cross over the road and take the right-hand road at the Y-junction towards **Bucklebury**. (You can also start from the roadside car park at the Bucklebury turning on the Upper Bucklebury–Chapel Row road (SU556692) or the Victory Room car park in Bucklebury (SU552707).) After 200m

Countryside near Bucklebury

turn left along a track through the trees of **Chapelrow Common** for about ¾ mile (1.1km) following the power-line poles. Turn right along a track (SU559693), passing a house (Bucklethwaite) on the left. Shortly after turn half-right at a small post and follow the steep path down through the wood to pass between two small ponds. Follow the track first right, then left up through the wood, to reach a narrow lane close to a large house. Turn right downhill, and just before the house on the right turn left along a track, firstly going down through the woodland and later climbing to reach a staggered junction. Continue almost straight on along the bridleway, slightly over to the right, and turn right along the track, passing a house. Follow the sunken track downhill, eventually crossing onto the other side of the hedge down to a stile.

② **SU551708** Turn right along the road towards **Bucklebury**, and shortly after passing the junction bear left through **St Mary the Virgin**'s churchyard, keeping left of the church, and go through the two small gates either side of a lane.

Bucklebury, originally recorded as Borchedeberie in the Domesday Book, is situated close to the River Pang: a cluster of cottages, interesting church and an old vicarage. The village rose in prominence when Reading Abbey built a manor house here for the abbot. However, with Henry VIII's dissolution of the monasteries the manor was sold to one John Winchcombe, son of the famous Jack of Newbury, who had made his wealth in the cloth trade. By 1703 the male line of the family had died out, so the manor passed to Frances Winchcombe, wife of Lord

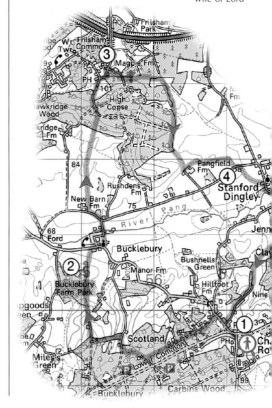

Bolingbroke, who later deserted his wife and fled to France. Unfortunately the Elizabethan manor house was extensively damaged by fire in 1830 and was later demolished, apart from one wing, which today forms part of Bucklebury House.

The 11th-century church of St Mary the Virgin has some impressive features, including an elaborately carved Norman doorway, high Georgian box pews and six interesting hatchments – coats of arms on diamond-shaped frames. The east window in the chancel depicting the Crucifixion, by Sir Frank Brangwyn (1867–1956), is unusual for both its striking colours and in that Christ is looking up to heaven, rather than down at the ground. Look out for the curious 'fly-window' in the chancel.

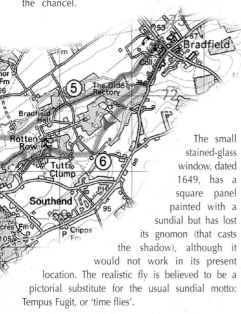

The small stained-glass window, dated 1649, has a square panel painted with a sundial but has lost its gnomon (that casts the shadow), although it would not work in its present location. The realistic fly is believed to be a pictorial substitute for the usual sundial motto: Tempus Fugit, or 'time flies'.

Cross the field, go through the kissing gate and continue northwards along the road crossing the **River Pang**. At the junction go up to the left, and shortly before **New Barn Farm** turn right, cross a stile and over the field, cross another stile and follow the track gently uphill. At the top corner of the large field bear slightly left through the scrub to cross several stiles and narrow fields in quick succession. Continue up across the wider field and cross another stile to follow the path up through the wood. Turn left along the track, and at the junction continue straight on down the lane. Follow the road to the right passing the **Pot Kiln**, ignore the path on the right, and instead turn right along a track towards **Magpie Farm**.

③ **SU554732** Follow the track round to the right, passing the farm buildings. At the track junction keep ahead along a footpath, up through the plantation, and bear left along a grassy track at the footpath sign. Go through the gate in the high fence and keep straight on through another gate, then immediately turn right and keep close to the fence on your right. Go left over a stile to follow the left-hand field boundary, keeping the trees on your left. On reaching a bridleway coming from the left, bear diagonally right across the field to a small gate.

Continue diagonally across the field to a sign in the fence ahead and turn right, to reach the field corner. Go through the gate and follow the narrow track for slightly over ½ mile (0.8km). At the cross-junction follow the permissive footpath (farm track) in the field on the left, following the boundary on the right; note the official bridleway continues straight ahead between the trees. Just before **Pangfield Farm** turn left along a signed path, past several farm buildings before following the path right and left, keeping close to the fence on the right. Continue through the stand of trees and cross the stile, following the path along the left boundary round two sides of the field, to cross a stile near **Severals Farm**.

④ **SU571719** Follow the lane left for 70m, and turn right along a footpath, keeping close to the right-hand field boundary. At the corner, cross two stiles a few metres apart and go diagonally over the field to

Typical scenery in the Pang Valley

cross another stile. Keep ahead through the next field aiming for the white weather-boarded tower of **St Denys' Church** to reach a stile and gate in the far corner.

The name of the picturesque village of **Stanford Dingley** is derived from the original lord of the manor, William de Stanford, and the Dyneley family who lived here in the Middle Ages. The church is unusual in that it is dedicated to St Denys, who was martyred in 3rd-century France; legend has it that his body stood up, picked up his head and walked through the streets to his chosen burial spot. The church has Saxon origins, though mostly dates from the 12th and 13th centuries; fragments of 13th-century wall paintings are still visible. A more recent addition is the engraved memorial window to the novelist and poet Robert Gathorne-Hardy (1902–73), who lived at Mill House for many years. Another well-to-do resident was Thomas Tesdale (1547–1610) who, from his personal fortune, co-founded Pembroke College in Oxford.

Go right along the road through **Stanford Dingley** and take the footpath opposite **The Bull**, going between the wooden seats and fence and past the old mill (now a private house) straddling the **River Pang** and later the Georgian Garden House. On reaching the road near to **The Old Boot**, turn left for a short distance.

Shorter walk
Turn right up the road towards Jennetts Hill for about 400m and then right along a path – continue with the route near to the end of Point 6.

Cross straight over at the junction to take a path along the valley bottom for just under 1 mile (1.6km), passing through several gates and ignoring any cross-paths/tracks to eventually reach a road.

⑤ **SU591719** Go right for a short distance and then left through a kissing gate, following a path with the woodland and field boundary on the left, after passing through another gate the path eventually follows the **River Pang** towards **Bradfield**, with Bradfield College to the right. At the village follow the path to the right and left, passing **St Andrew's Church** and later the old mill and picturesque riverside cottages.

Bradfield, whose name simply means 'broad field', was first mentioned in a Saxon document. Most of what you see today is down to the efforts of one man: the Reverend Thomas Stevens, a former Victorian rector. Stevens was also responsible for the opening of a mineral water plant at St Andrew's Well, and the introduction of one of the first milking machines to the area.

The Bull pub in Stanford Dingley

St Andrew's Church, which dates back to the early 1300s, was originally dedicated to St John the Baptist, but rededicated to St Andrew in 1848 after extensive enlargement by Stevens, with the help of his friend, the leading Victorian Gothic Revival architect Sir George Gilbert Scott (1811–78). Gilbert Scott was responsible for designing such famous structures as the Midland Grand Hotel at St Pancras Station and the Albert Memorial, both in London. However, Stevens found it difficult to fill the pews, so he established St Andrew's School in 1850 – now Bradfield College – to provide a choir and larger congregation. As the school grew to dominate the village, and Stevens' other ventures drained his financial resources, he was declared bankrupt and the school taken over by a board of trustees, who employed Dr Herbert Gray as headmaster. It was Dr Gray who turned Bradfield College into one of the best schools in the area.

At the main road go up to the right and then right again at the crossroads following the road for Bucklebury and Southend. Keep to the pavement on the right past the college church, and then continue along the road for about 300m (*care required*). Turn right at the metalled drive, signed for the Old Rectory, passing a cottage and, after 120m, turn left onto a path just to the left of the fence.

At the top corner go right over the stile, now following a fence and golf course on your left to cross another stile. Keep ahead through an avenue of trees with the golf course on either side; just before the buildings follow the path to the left for a short distance and then right through a gate in the hedge. Cross over the lane and through the gate ahead following a path over the field; continue through two gates to the left of the field corner. Keep ahead through the next field to a gate, and take the path diagonally left up through the middle of the field to a gate.

⑥ **SU595712** Cross straight over **Mariners Lane** and follow the path over the stile and then diagonally right along a narrow fenced path between the fields (PYO fruit and veg). Go over a stile and continue across the field to cross two stiles a few metres apart. Cross straight over the lane and follow the signed path through **Stanford Wood**, passing under a small brick bridge. Turn left up the road at **Rotten Row** and then right at the junction through **Tutts Clump**, later passing the Methodist church on the left. Just before Kimber House turn right down a narrow path between the houses and through the trees to reach a broad track, with a fence ahead. Turn left along the track, ignoring paths off to left and right, keeping to the bridleway as it bears right then left.

Turn right down the road at **Jennetts Hill** for 100m and then left along a path passing a house and garage (**shorter walk rejoins here**). Go through a kissing gate, and follow the fence on the right to another kissing gate and keep straight ahead. At the far side of the field turn left uphill, following the hedge on the right; later the track follows the left-hand edge of the woodland before passing some houses. Turn left along the road back to Chapel Row.

WALK 16

Dorchester-on-Thames:
An Ancient Place of Worship

Distance	11 miles (17.7km)
Time	4¾ hours
Grade	1
Map	OS Explorer 170/Landranger 174
Start/finish	Car park at Wittenham Clumps, about 1 mile (1.6km) off A4130 at Brightwell-cum-Sotwell (SU567924)
Public transport	Thames Travel buses from Wallingford and Oxford stop at Dorchester-on-Thames
Refreshments	Dorchester-on-Thames – local shops; The George Hotel (01865 340404); Fleur de Lys (01865 340502); White Hart Hotel (01865 340074); Long Wittenham – The Vyne (01865 407832); The Plough Inn (01865 407738)

This walk starts with some panoramic views from the Wittenham Clumps (Sinodun Hills), one of which is crowned by the remains of an Iron Age hill-fort. From there it heads down to cross the Thames at Little Wittenham and visits the historic former Roman town of Dorchester-on-Thames with its Augustinian abbey. The return leg follows the gentle riverside path alongside the Thames to the village of Long Wittenham with its famous model railway museum before returning to the car park.

A figure-of-eight walk in southern Oxfordshire following in the footsteps of poets, painters and pilgrims.

① **SU567924** From the car park turn right up the track, through the right-hand gate and bear slightly right up through the ramparts of **Castle Hill** fort. Walk anti-clockwise partway round the earth ramparts and then across the middle, passing just north of a stand of trees and a large memorial stone commemorating the poem tree.

The unusual twin tops of the **Wittenham Clumps**, Castle Hill and Round Hill, are crowned by stands of

Round Hill – one of the Wittenham Clumps

beech trees and offer some great views over Oxfordshire and Chilterns. The 'clumps' are also known as the Sinodun Hills, the name being derived from the Celtic *seno dunum*, meaning 'old fort'; Castle Hill is crowned with the remains of an Iron Age hill-fort. Both summits are now part of the Little Wittenham Nature Reserve, set up by the Northmoor Trust in 1982. Castle Hill is also known for the Poem Tree; the epic poem was carved into the tree in 1844–45 by Joseph Tubb of Warborough Green:

> *As up the hill with labr'ing steps we tread*
> *Where the twin Clumps their sheltering*
>   *branches spread*
> *The summit gain'd at ease reclining lay*
> *And all around the wide spread scene survey*
> *Point out each object and instructive tell*
> *The various changes that the land befell.*

Although you can't visit the tree, there is a memorial stone on the north side of the trees commemorating the 150th anniversary of the carving of the poem. The 'clumps' have been captured often on canvas and film, most famously in the landscape artist Paul Nash's (1889–1946) *Landscape on a Vernal Equinox* in 1944.

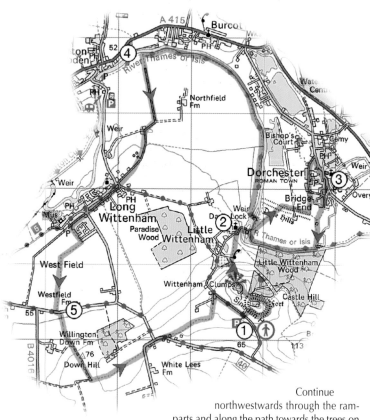

Continue northwestwards through the ramparts and along the path towards the trees on the other hilltop, **Round Hill**. Follow the path round to reach the seats next to the view indicator, with excellent views over the Thames Valley. Head north down the steep slope, passing a gate, and keep ahead to another gate at **Little Wittenham**.

The 14th-century church of St Peter in **Little Wittenham** was originally dedicated to St Faith, a martyr from the

south of France, who was burnt to death. Inside is a fine
17th-century memorial to Sir William Dunch, MP for
Wallingford in the 1560s, and a figure of his wife, Mary
Dunch, an aunt of Oliver Cromwell.

② **SU566934** Turn right along the lane, passing **St
Peter's Church**, and then cross the bridges over the River
Thames at **Day's Lock**.

> The bridge over the river by the lock-keeper's cottage
> at **Days Lock** is the site of the famous World Pooh
> Sticks Championships, and 2008 marks the 25th
> anniversary of the event. Based on the game made
> famous by Winnie the Pooh and his friends in a book
> written by A.A. Milne (1882–1956), the event raises
> money for both the RLNI and many good causes sup-
> ported by the Rotary Club of Sinodun.

Go through the gate and head diagonally left across the
field for 200m to reach a small gate. Follow the narrow
hedge-lined path and cross over **Dyke Hills**.

> The **Dyke Hills** earthworks are thought to be from the
> Iron Age, and form part of a promontory settlement
> protected on three sides by the Rivers Thames and
> Thame, with a double rampart – the Dyke Hills – on
> the north side.

Bear right and walk beside the fence with the earthworks
on the right. Continue along the track, ignoring the first
track off to the left, and at the next track turn left towards
Dorchester-on-Thames. Follow the path between the gardens to join Watling Lane (track) and go straight on for
500m to reach the war memorial. Turn sharp right along
the High Street, passing the **White Hart Hotel**, and at **The
George Hotel** turn left through the lych-gate, passing the
museum and tea room, to visit **Dorchester Abbey**.

> The Romans built a settlement at **Dorchester-on-Thames**
> on their route between Silchester and Alchester. In

AD635, on the banks of the Thames, Oswald of Northumbria, overlord of the Anglo-Saxon kingdoms, met Cynegils, King of Wessex, to celebrate his marriage to Cynegils' daughter. Part of the arrangement was that the pagan king would become a Christian, with the baptism being conducted by Birinus, a missionary sent by the Pope. This helped the spread of Christianity in England, and Dorchester-on-Thames became – and still is – an important religious centre. As a reward, Birinus was given permission to build his Saxon cathedral church, but after the Norman Conquest the See was moved to Lincoln, and in 1140 the old church was re-founded as an Augustinian abbey.

The Abbey Church of St Peter and St Paul has a striking 14th-century Tree of Jesse window, and a fine Norman lead font. The earliest glass in the abbey (c. 1225) can be seen in the Birinus Chapel. There are also some wonderful effigies, including a Crusader knight, thought by many to be one of the best pieces of 13th-century funerary sculpture in England. In the Lady Chapel are other effigies, including one of John de Stonor (d. 1354), Lord Chief Justice of England under Edward III, whose descendants live at nearby Stonor House (see Walk 22). There are also some medieval wall paintings, and the Cloister Gallery tells the story of the abbey through a collection of medieval stonework – all that survives of the monastic buildings that were destroyed in the 16th century.

The tea room and museum is next door in the former monastery guest house and grammar school building, dating from the 1400s (museum and tea room open on Saturday and Sunday afternoons from May to end of September, and some weekdays; 01865 340751).

③ **SU579942** On leaving the abbey go southwards along the Rose Walk path to reach a small gate next to the octagonal toll-house on the right (built at the same time as the bridge over the River Thame, and in operation until 1873). Cross over the road and continue along Bridge End Road, signposted for the car park and

The Augustinian Abbey Church of St Peter and St Paul at Dorchester-on-Thames

public conveniences, later passing the Roman Catholic **Church of St Birinus** ▶ Shortly after passing the church, turn right into Watling Lane and immediately go left along Wittenham Lane, signposted 'River and Wittenham 1¼'. Continue along the lane and at the right-hand bend, next to the last building, leave the track and go straight on along the left side of the field. Cross the stile and go past Dyke Hills heading south, go through another field and turn right along the **Thames Path**. Shortly after going under Little Wittenham Bridge turn left over **Days Lock** and weir, signposted 'Clifton Hampden 3', and bear right following the Thames Path for just over 2 miles (3.2km) to reach **Clifton Meadow**, a flood meadow cared for by the Northmoor Trust.

This small church was built in 1849 by W.W. Wardell, who later emigrated to Australia and built the great Catholic cathedrals in Sydney and Melbourne.

④ **SU553958** At the far side of **Clifton Meadow** stay in the same field, and turn left along a path, following the fence on the right and using the raised wooden walkway. Go through the gate and keep ahead along the track, following it to the right and then half-left at **New Barn Farm**, ignoring the path off to the left, and continuing towards **Long Wittenham**. On reaching the road bear first right and then left to head along the High Street past **St Mary's Church** and two pubs: **The Vyne** and **The Plough Inn**.

St Mary's Church at **Long Wittenham** was built in 1120 by the Norman lord of the manor Walter Gifford, 3rd Earl of Buckingham. Inside is a rare example of a 12th-century lead font, and a small stone effigy of a knight, said to be the smallest sculptured monument in England. The figure is of Gilbert de Clare ('Gilbert the Red'), lord of the manor of Long Wittenham and Earl of Gloucester and Hertfordshire, who died during the Crusades to the Holy Lands in 1295.

The River Thames near Long Wittenham

At the junction, next to the village cross, keep ahead for 300m to a junction with a lane on the left, next to the

post office and shop (SU543935). If you want to visit the **Pendon Museum** continue straight on for 50m from here.

> **Pendon Museum** houses several model train settings, including one of rural Berkshire in the 1920s and 1930s. The most famous is the Madder Valley model railway, built by John Ahern who, during the 1930s, pioneered the idea of setting model railways in a scenic landscape (open most Saturday and Sunday afternoons; 01865 407365).

If not, turn left along the lane between the houses, go straight over at the junction with the lane – **Fieldside** – and follow the path, keeping the buildings on the left. At the field corner follow the path to the right and then left, crossing a footbridge. Continue straight on with the field boundary on the left to reach a road.

⑤ **SU542924** Turn left for 75m and then right along a footpath with the field boundary on the right. Go through the gate and continue through the next field to reach a gate and stile. Cross over and bear first right and then left, following the left-hand edge of the field up **Down Hill**, to the top field corner. Turn left into the next field and follow the path, keeping close to the boundary on the right. Bear slightly left along the road for 350m, ignoring the road off to the left. Where the road bends to the right, turn left along a signed path through the trees to cross a stile. Go right along the field boundary next to the high hedge and telegraph poles, cross the stile and keep ahead, with the fence on the right to another stile. Follow the track as it bears left and passes to the right of the buildings at **Hill Farm** and the recently opened Project Timescape, Northmoor Trust's new education and visitor centre. Turn right along the road for 450m back to the car park.

WALK 17

The Aldworth Giants and Thurle Down

Distance	12½ miles (20.1km)
Time	5½ hours
Grade	2
Map	OS Explorers 159 and 170/Landranger 174 and 175
Start/finish	National Trust car park at Lardon Chase, Streatley (SU583807); alternative start at Goring railway station (SU602806)
Public transport	Thames Travel bus from Wallingford stops at Streatley/Goring; trains to Goring (short walk)
Refreshments	Streatley – Bull at Streatley (01491 872392); Moulsford – Beetle and Wedge (01491 651381); Aldworth – Bell Inn (01635 578272)

Walk in giant's footsteps on a day of discovery in the rolling Berkshire Downs to the west of the Goring Gap, where the River Thames flows between the Berkshire Downs and the Chilterns. From the heights of Lardon Chase with its far-reaching views over rolling Chiltern scenery, the route descends to follow the Thames for a couple of miles before climbing back into the downs to reach the little Berkshire village of Aldworth – a place where giants sleep. The small, Norman Church of St Mary is rightly famous for its collection of nine giant stone effigies of the de la Beche family, dating from the 14th century. The route then heads back to Lardon Chase.

This walk can also be started from Goring railway station, ¼ mile (1.2km) to the east, across the River Thames, from the turning to St Mary's Church in Streatley.

① **SU583807** Go through the small gate in the northeast corner of the car park, following the trees and hedge on the left over **Lardon Chase** (National Trust), with views over the Goring Gap. Near the end of the broad ridge, where the hedge turns sharp left, bear half-right downhill towards the field corner. Go through a small gate and bear right down a gravel track, then turn left down the road (B4009) towards Streatley. Go

straight over the crossroads next to the **Bull at Streatley** and down the High Street for 300m. Goring railway station, from where the walk can also be started, is across the Thames.

Looking towards the Chilterns from Lardon Chase above the Goring Gap

> **Streatley** village has a history dating from Anglo-Saxon times. Following the Norman Conquest, Geoffrey de Manderville was lord of Streatley Manor. St Mary's Church was largely rebuilt in 1864 and has some interesting brasses dating from the 15th to 17th centuries. The Bull, at the crossroads on the A329, is where Jerome K. Jerome's *Three Men in a Boat* had lunch. Streatley House in the High Street dates from 1765 and was once the home of the Morrell family (brewers in Oxford).

Turn left at Childe Court and go along the lane passing **St Mary's Church**, signposted 'Moulsford 2½', following the **Thames Path** to Moulsford. On reaching the **Beetle and Wedge** turn left at the gate and go through the car park, then left along **Ferry Lane** to the main road (A329).

The unusual name of the Beetle and Wedge restaurant and hotel at **Moulsford** is derived from an 18th-century practice of splitting trees into planks, which where then floated downriver; the beetle, or mallet, was used to drive wedges into the trees to split them. Author H.G. Wells stayed here in 1910 while writing his novel *The History of Mr Polly*; the pub features in the book as the Potwell Inn.

② **SU592836** Go right for about 170m and turn left, crossing the road, to follow the gravel track between two cottages, **Pye Corner** and **Mead Corner**. Keep ahead along the metalled lane between the houses, and where the lane bends sharply left, turn right along a signed footpath with the houses on the right and wire fence and field on the left. At the fence corner, with the large playing field on the right, turn left following the narrow overgrown path next to the wire fence (you can follow the left-hand side of the field on the right through the trees if necessary). On reaching the fence turn left and then immediately right through a gap and bear right into the field, following the left-

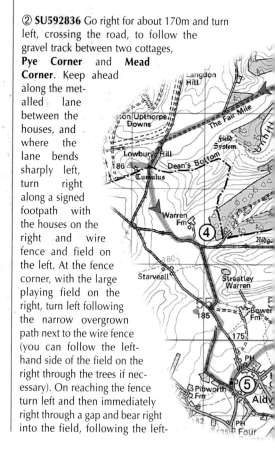

hand field boundary gently uphill. Shortly after passing under the large power lines go through the gap in the hedge on the left (posts with yellow arrows), and then right, following the field edge on the right. Follow the path left for about 50m and then right uphill, keeping close to the trees, later going over the field to reach the **Wantage road** (A417).

③ **SU577836** Turn right uphill, keeping on the wide verge; at the brow of the hill turn left, crossing the road (*care required*) and follow the track signposted to the downs. Ignore the

Near the top of the rise, where the track bends left, take a short detour to **Lowbury Hill**, open under the DEFRA Conservation Walks scheme. To visit the summit turn right and go through two gates following the fence on the right, later walking to the trig point for a great view.

track down to the left, but keep straight on to follow the right-hand track up through the trees and along **The Fair Mile**, a horse gallop. At the cross-tracks (SU544826) turn left up along a track (byway). ◄ Continue up the track for 150m from the detour point and at the footpath sign go through the gap in the hedge on the left to follow a path for 750m, firstly along the grassy strip between fields and later with the hedge on the right. Continue along the track – the **Ridgeway** – passing the entrance to **Warren Farm**.

④ **SU549813** At the junction leave the Ridgeway and turn right along the byway for 750m; to the left are great views over **Streatley Warren** to the Chilterns. Follow the track round to the right and then go left along Ambury Road towards **Aldworth** for 250m. Go right along a track, which becomes Townsend Road. Follow it as it turns left to pass **Dumworth Farm**, later bear right and, at the junction, turn sharp left to enter **St Mary's** churchyard via the small gate.

Aldworth is a picturesque village that was known as Elleorde, the 'Old Town', at the time of the Domesday Book. St Mary's Church, which dates back to Norman times, is famed for the 'Aldworth Giants', nine 14th-century larger-than-life effigies of the de la Beche family. The family came to England in the wake of William the Conqueror and built the castle of de la Beche nearby, though this has long since disappeared; the present de la Beche Farm is built on the site. During excavations in 1871 a silver seal bearing the name Isabella de la Beche was found, now held in Reading Museum.

The first of the stone figures along the north wall is that of Sir Robert de la Beche, then his son Sir John, and in turn his son Sir Philip. Although Sir Philip was valet to Edward II he took part in a rebellion in 1322, led by the Earl of Lancaster, to overthrow the king. The uprising ended at the Battle of Boroughbridge in Yorkshire; Sir Philip was imprisoned and his lands confiscated. Five years later, Isabella of France (once

Looking over Streatley Warren to the Chilterns

queen to Edward II), returned to England with her son who became Edward III; he later restored Sir Philip to the manor at Aldworth.

In the nave are Sir John and his wife Lady Isabella, then Lord Nicholas. The male line of the de la Beche family came to an end with the death of Lord Nicholas in 1348, though the family held the manor for another 150 years in the female line of Langford. Lord Nicholas' elder brother Sir Philip lies with his sister Lady Joan along the south aisle with John, son of Lady Isabella.

In 1644, Colonel Symonds, an officer of King Charles I, made notes on the effigies, from which it is known that the three figures with missing heads were still intact. The damage was probably done in the 1650s when Cromwell's 'army' visited the church. By the 17th century local people had given names to four of the figures; the largest was known as John Long, the others as John Strong, John Never Afraid and John Ever Afraid. The latter, which has disappeared, is said to have promised his soul to the Devil, whether he was buried inside or outside the church. However, he tricked the Devil by being buried in the wall, so neither inside nor outside the church.

The area has connections with two poets: Alfred Lord Tennyson and Laurence Binyon. In 1850 Tennyson (1809–92) married Emily Sellwood, whose family home was nearby Pibworth Manor, at Shiplake (see Walk 23). The ashes of Laurence Binyon (1869–1943), who lived for a while at Westridge Farm, are buried in the churchyard with those of his wife Cecily. He is especially remembered for his poem *For the Fallen* (1914):

> *They shall not grow old, as we that are left grow old:*
>
> *Age shall not weary them, nor the years condemn.*
>
> *At the going down of the sun and in the morning We will remember them.*

Leave through the lych-gate in the northeast corner and follow the lane towards the village, bearing right at the Y-junction to reach the **Bell Inn**. On the right is an old well constructed in 1868, claimed to be one of the deepest in England at 113m (372ft).

⑤ **SU556796** Go to the right past the pub for a few metres, and at the phone box turn left to follow an enclosed path; later keep ahead across the field. Go through the gap in the hedge and, ignoring the crossing path, continue across the next field. Turn right along the track, later a metalled lane, and keep ahead along the B4009 through **Westridge Green** for 300m. Turn left at the entrance to **Westridge Farm** and follow the track past the farm buildings and down the hill, passing **Kiddington Cottage**, to eventually reach a road. Turn right for 650m, and after a slight rise turn right at the footpath sign along an enclosed path next to a large farm gate. Cross the stile and metalled track and follow the path up across the golf course (*care required* – ring the warning bells where available), keeping just to the left of the first patch of scrub and right of the second. At the top of the hill pass just to the right of the green and leave the golf course by the gap in the hedge to reach the car park.

Effigy of Lord Nicholas de la Beche in St Mary's Church at Aldworth

163

WALK 18
The Goring Challenge

Distance	16 miles (25.7km) or 8½ miles (13.7km)
Time	6¾ hours or 4 hours
Grade	2
Map	OS Explorer 171/Landranger 175
Start/finish	Car park off Station Road, Goring (SU599807); alternative start at Goring railway station (SU602806)
Public transport	Trains to Goring; Thames Travel buses from Wallingford to Goring
Refreshments	Goring – shops; Miller of Mansfield (01491 872829); The John Barleycorn (01491 872509); Catherine Wheel (01491 872379); Queens Arms (01491 872825); Mapledurham House – tea room (when house is open); Whitchurch-on-Thames – (short detour) Greyhound (0118 984 2160); Ferryboat Inn (0118 984 2161)

This fairly long walk of 16 miles (25.7km) starts from the riverside town of Goring and heads through typical Chiltern countryside of beech woods and rolling fields before descending back towards the River Thames. Make sure you have time to look around Mapledurham with its house, mill and church, which have starred in many big screen and TV productions. The return route follows the peaceful Thames Path upstream to Goring.

This walk can also be started at Goring railway station (SU602806).

① **SU599807** From the car park walk back to **Station Road** and turn left. At the T-junction go left into **Red Cross Road** and then right along the **High Street** to cross the railway bridge. Turn right along Wallingford Road towards the railway station (*alternative start point SU602806*). At the junction, next to the **Queens Arms**, go up along the B4526 for a short distance and then right into Whitehills Green (cul-de-sac). Follow the pavement up through the estate, and at the top go right along a

Gatepost detail at Mapledurham

path between the hedges and gardens and through a gate to reach the playing fields.

Cross diagonally left to another gate and turn left through two fields, keeping to the boundary on the left. At the field corner follow the path down and cross the stile on the left before heading uphill; cross another stile and keep ahead up through **Great Chalk Wood**. Turn right up the signed bridleway, and near the top of the wood bear left through a gate and past some buildings on your left. Go through the next gate and turn left under the power lines to another gate. Turn right along the lane past **Cold Harbour** to reach the road (B471).

Shorter walk

At Cold Harbour turn right over a stile (SU632796) and follow the left-hand path across the field; cross a stile in the corner and continue across the next field to the left of buildings. Turn right along the road for 75m and then left at the farm entrance; continue between buildings and then half-right through trees, passing a kissing gate; after passing the next gate rejoin the main route at SU634788 (see Point 5).

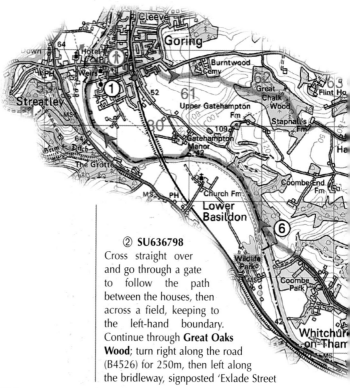

② **SU636798**

Cross straight over and go through a gate to follow the path between the houses, then across a field, keeping to the left-hand boundary. Continue through **Great Oaks Wood**; turn right along the road (B4526) for 250m, then left along the bridleway, signposted 'Exlade Street

1½', through **Oaken Wood**, keeping straight on at the junction with a cross-path. ▶ Keep ahead over the road and along the signed bridleway through **Common Wood**. At the waymarked crossing, near to the field corner on your left (SU654808), turn right along another bridleway. Continue ahead at the next crossing and follow the bridleway through **Bensgrove Wood** to eventually reach the B4526.

③ **SU663800** Cross straight over and take the bridleway, signed for 'Nuney Green ¾', through **Hawhill Wood**, passing some fields on your left. Where the wood starts again continue straight on, keeping the wire fence and Little College Wood on your left.

This section can be difficult to follow – look out for the white arrows on the trees.

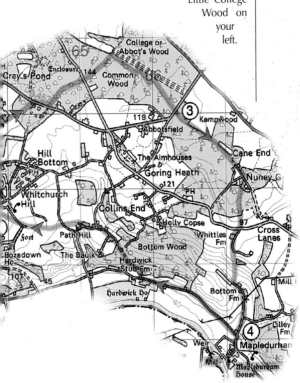

*The water mill at
Mapledurham*

Follow the path between the ponds and continue along the bridleway, becoming enclosed between hedges, to join a lane at **Nuney Green**. Keep ahead at the junction, and at the far end of the garden on the right (50m past junction) turn half-right along a path signposted 'Mapledurham 1½', keeping the fence and later a tall fir hedge on the right. Continue ahead through **Nuney Wood** and, at the far side, go through the kissing gate and follow the path over the field, keeping between the fence and a line of trees.

Go through the kissing gate and turn right along the lane for a few metres before turning left to pass **Whittles Farm**. Leave the lane where it bends to the left and cross the stile in the fence on the right. Follow the left-hand hedge and fence downhill – good views across the valley. Cross the stile and continue downhill to the gate in the left-hand corner of the field. Turn left along the farm track, later a concrete track, passing **Bottom Farm** to join a road at a bend. Turn right towards **Mapledurham** for 250m to reach **The White House** on the right. If you have time, take a short detour down the road to visit **Mapledurham**.

The name of the secluded and picturesque riverside hamlet of **Mapledurham** is derived from the Saxon Mapledreham, 'homestead by the maple tree'. Along the village street are a number of 17th-century cottages, while at far end, down a short track on the right, is the 15th-century mill, the oldest working water mill on the Thames – you can still buy flour there. To the left is St Margaret's Church, built around 1200 and unusual in that it has a screened-off Catholic chapel, dating from the late 1300s. The chapel now belongs to the Eystons, heirs of the Blount family, the traditional Catholic owners of the Mapledurham estate. Parts of Mapledurham House date from the 15th century, though most of what is seen today results from rebuilding by Sir Michael Blount in 1588. The village was used as the location for the film *The Eagle has Landed*, when it was known as Studley Constable and based in Norfolk; the Spyglass and Kettle pub was a fake (there is no pub in the village). The village has also starred in numerous TV dramas including *The Forsyte Saga*, *The Wind in the Willows* and *Inspector Morse*. The house, tea shop and mill are open to the public at certain times (0118 972 3350).

Mapledurham House

④ **SU671770** From The White House follow the fenced bridleway, signposted 'Whitchurch 2½', eventually passing East Lodge and the entrance gate to Hardwick Park, and later reaching **Hardwick House**.

Built on foundations dating from about 1400, the present **Hardwick House** dates from the time of the Tudor politician Richard Lybbe, who entertained Queen Elizabeth I here. Charles I played bowls on the lawn shortly before the Civil War.

Just after Hardwick House turn right along a fenced track (bridleway – no sign) following it up through the trees, bearing left past the chalk pit and keeping to the main track ahead. Close to the top ignore the path off to the right and keep straight on, and after leaving the wood continue along the lane to pass **Path Hill Farm**. Turn left at the junction by some cottages at **Path Hill** to follow the road downhill. Just before the left-hand bend, bear slightly right along a track past the last house on the right. Keep ahead over a stile and follow the hedge along the right-hand edge of the field, cross a stile in the top corner and turn left along the enclosed track for 50m.

At the footpath sign go right into the field, keeping the hedge on your left, and then across the field to join a track by some trees. Continue straight on through the belt of trees, ignoring the path off to the right. Go along the track between the fields for 400m, turn half-left through a kissing gate and continue diagonally across the field to reach the corner of the fence. Follow the fence on the right through a kissing gate and continue along the fenced track past some houses to reach a road junction at **Whitchurch Hill**.

⑤ **SU638787** Cross over the road and village green. Turn right along the road (B471) passing **St John the Baptist Church**, and just after the **Goring Heath Parish Hall** turn left along a concrete track. Go through the gate and follow the field edge, keeping the trees on the right, to a junction next to a gate (SU634788) (**shorter walk rejoins here**). Turn left here across the field and through a gate to join a track passing to the left of **Beech Farm**; keep ahead along the enclosed track. Go through the gate and continue, keeping the field boundary and **Stonycroft Plantation** on your right, to the bottom of the field and a gate. Follow the path down to the war memorial, cross over the road and follow the raised pathway down towards **Whitchurch-on-Thames**, crossing back over at the end of the footpath. ▶ Go along the lane, signposted 'Thames Path Goring 3½ and Hartslock Bridleway', and where the lane turns sharply down to the left, keep ahead down some steps into a hollow and up the other side to reach **Hartslock Wood**.

If a pub stop is required continue down into the village for about 600m, then retrace the route back to this point.

> BBOWT **Hartslock Nature Reserve** covers a small area of unimproved chalk downland above Hartslock Wood (accessible from the Goring end), and is home to a range of plants and animals, including the rare monkey orchid, which typically flowers during May.

⑥ **SU622784** Continue down through the woodland and keep ahead along the fenced bridleway towards **Gatehampton Manor**. Turn left at the footpath sign, keeping to the Thames Path, and cross the footbridge, passing **Ferry Cottage**. Turn right, following the riverside path and passing under **Gatehampton railway bridge** (built by the renowned GWR engineer Isambard Kingdom Brunel in the 1830s) to reach the bridge at **Goring**. Turn right up the lane, and shortly after passing the **old water mill** turn right along another lane, bear left through a gate and continue through **St Thomas of Canterbury**'s churchyard.

> **Goring** is situated in the Goring Gap, where the River Thames flows between the Chiltern Hills and the Berkshire Downs. Goring has been a major crossing point over the Thames since Celtic times – the ancient Icknield Way crossed here – though the first bridge wasn't built until 1837. The mill, originally a corn mill, was converted to generate electricity at the end the 19th century and closed in 1927.

Green Man sculpture in St Thomas of Canterbury Church in Goring

The typically Norman church of St Thomas of Canterbury dates from around 1100 and was probably built by Robert d'Oilly, a Norman baron and staunch supporter of William the Conqueror, who held 60 manors including 'Garinges' (Goring). The church houses a bell cast in 1290 – believed to be one of the oldest in Britain – while the wooden rood screen is carved out of oak from HMS *Thunderer*, a bomb-ketch which fought under Nelson at the Battle of Trafalgar. The old water mill and church are depicted in an unfinished painting by Turner in 1805, now in the Tate Gallery, London. Oscar Wilde spent the summer of 1893 at Ferry Cottage (near Gatehampton Manor), and his play *An Ideal Husband* includes references to the area. The cottage was later the home of Air Marshall Arthur 'Bomber' Harris of Dambusters fame, until his death in 1984.

Turn right along Manor Road – the **Miller of Mansfield** can be seen to the left – pass the **John Barleycorn** and turn left along **Station Road**, then left again at the **Catherine Wheel** to arrive back at the car park.

Alternative start/finish
If you need the railway station continue along Station Road, then left along Red Cross Road, right along the High Street crossing the railway bridge, then right along Wallingford Road.

WALK 19

Oxford Hills and the River Thame

Distance	12½ miles (20.1km)
Time	5½ hours
Grade	2
Map	OS Explorers 170 and 180/Landranger 163
Start/finish	Roundabout close to Stadhampton church at junction of A329 and B480 (SU604988); parking at edge of village green just off B480
Public transport	Bus links to Oxford and Wheatley from Little Milton, Cuddesdon and Garsington
Refreshments	Cuddesdon – Bat and Ball (01865 874379); Garsington – Three Horseshoes (01865 361395); The Red Lion (01865 361413); Toot Baldon – The Mole Inn (01865 340001); Chiselhampton – The Coach & Horses (01865 890255); Stadhampton – The Crown (01865 890381)

This fairly long walk starts from the village of Stadhampton, with its large village green and unusual church tower, and heads across open farmland to the village of Little Milton before descending to the River Thame at Cuddesdon Mill. The route then heads for the hilltop villages of Cuddesdon, Garsington and Toot Baldon in the Oxfordshire Hills to the southeast of Oxford. The final leg of the route passes Chiselhampton, crossing over the River Thame – which starts life north of Aylesbury and joins the River Thames at Dorchester – to reach Stadhampton.

Stadhampton The large village green is surrounded by many interesting cottages and houses, as well as the 13th-century parish church of St John the Baptist. The church has a Norman font and several brasses, and a tower adorned by four large urns, added in 1737. A famous son of the village was the Puritan church leader and theologian John Owen (1616–83).

Several pubs are visited during this walk – just make sure you don't stop at each one!

① **SU604988** Walk towards the village along the A329 for a few metres, and then left along a signed path over the village green, following the houses on the right. Cross over the lane – **Cat Lane** – go through the kissing gate and ahead along a path through the trees. On reaching a hedge cross a stile on the right and continue with the field boundary on the left; later keep ahead across the middle of the field. Go through the belt of trees, ignoring the crossing bridleway, and go over the stile to follow the line of trees ahead through **Ascott Park** (the official path is on the right of the wire fence) towards the farm; on the right is the dovecot, to the left the gateposts.

> Little is known about the history of **Ascott Park** except that in 1662 Sir William Dormer built a grand house in the park, which burnt down before construction was complete; thereafter the site was abandoned. All that remains today are the traces of earthworks and odd historic buildings, including a late 16th-century brick-built dovecot, icehouse, and late 17th-century gate piers alongside the B480. The parkland overlies the remains of the medieval hamlet of Ascott.

At the farm cross the stile to the right of the gate and continue through the farmyard, passing another gate, and turn left along the lane. Cross straight over the road (B480) and continue along the metalled track, signposted 'Little Milton 1¾'. After passing the entrance to **Belcher's Farm** keep ahead along the gravel track and eventually go through a large metal gate. Follow the field edge on the right to the corner, and continue across the field heading north and aiming for the church in the distance.

At the far side of the field cross the footbridge and stile in the trees and keep ahead through the next field, again aiming for the church and passing under two sets of power lines to cross a footbridge and stile. Keep ahead across the third field aiming for the house, cross the stile in the fence and follow the enclosed path past the houses to the road (A329) at **Little Milton**.

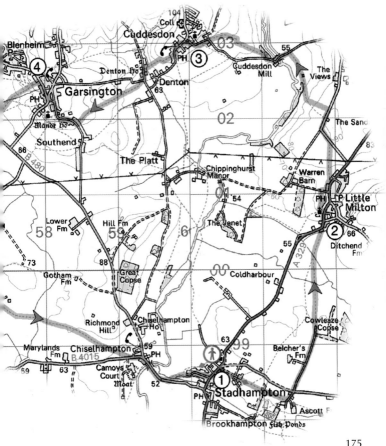

Old icehouse and dovecot at Ascott Park

② **SU618005** Turn right, passing the school and Gold Street, cross at the traffic lights and continue up to the **Parish Church of St James** built in 1843; opposite are two tiny picturesque thatched cottages. Turn left along an enclosed path at the end of the churchyard and then right along a track, with a house to the right. Go through the kissing gate and turn right along the track for a few metres before turning left along a track with gardens to the right and field to the left (*permissive route – not official right of way – right of way is off the main street*). Follow the path towards the hedge – but do not go through to the sports ground – and bear left to the end of the hedge. Now go diagonally over the field, passing to the right of the pylon, to cross a stile in the hedge.

Turn left along the lane for 200m and follow it round to the right for 150m, then turn left through a gate opposite the house (notice the DEFRA sign for Conservation Walks). (*The official right of way goes diagonally right down across to fields to a stile in the hedge on the right.*) The permissive path goes right following the field edge, and after passing through a gap in the hedge turns left downhill with the hedge to the left (*later the official route joins from the left*). Continue down the field, and at the bottom turn right through the trees and past a gate. Keep ahead through a kissing gate and pass a wooden building, and continue through the next field to a small gate.

Turn left along the lane to pass **Cuddesdon Mill** and cross the **River Thame**, continue up round to the right and, where the lane bends slightly left, cross the stile on the right and follow the path up across the field, aiming to the right of the church in **Cuddesdon**. Go through the hedge/fence and keep ahead, later turning left across the field to cross a stile in the fence. Continue through the trees to cross a further two stiles a metre apart and turn right up the road, passing a pond on the left. Keep left at the junction; **All Saints Church** is a short distance up to the right.

Cuddesdon is one of several picturesque stone-built villages in the Oxford Hills between Oxford and the Thames Valley. All Saints Church, which is visible for miles around, was built around 1180 at the behest of Abingdon Abbey, and enjoys a superb view over rolling countryside out towards Buckinghamshire. The west entrance is particularly impressive. The village is probably better known as the home of Ripon College, built in 1854 for Bishop Wilberforce of Oxford by the young Wantage-born architect G.E. Street, who went on to design the Law Courts in London.

③ **SU600030** Follow the High Street past the **Bat and Ball**, which is crammed with an eclectic array of cricketing memorabilia. At Denton Hill road turn right along a signed metalled path past Style Cottage, cross the stile and continue downhill with the fence on the right. Cross the stile in the corner and continue downhill to another stile, go over the footbridge and turn left along the lane passing **Denton House** (hidden behind the high wall).

Turn right at the junction for 110m, then left at the stile; go diagonally over the field to cross another stile, and keep ahead up through three fields to eventually reach a gate and stile in **Garsington**.

> The manor house at **Garsington** (not open to the public) is largely 16th century, and was built by William Wickham; it was here that Oliver Cromwell (1599–1658) and Sir Thomas Fairfax (1612–71) met to plot the siege of Oxford during the Civil War. During World War I and through the 1920s the manor house was home to Lady Ottoline Morrell (d. 1938), sister of the Duke of Portland, who married Philip Morrell (of the famous Oxford brewing family). Lady Ottoline and her husband invited many of the leading artists, literary and intellectual figures of the day to Garsington, and the house became a sanctuary for the likes of John Maynard Keynes, Virginia Woolf, T.S. Eliot, Bertrand Russell, Aldous Huxley and poet Siegfried Sassoon.
>
> The author H. Rider Haggard also lived at Garsington in his youth, and used the surname of a local farmer for his hero Allan Quartermain in *King Solomon's Mines*; Garsington became 'Garsingham', Quartermain's birthplace. In 1982 Leonard and Rosalind Ingrams acquired the house, and in 1989 they founded the famous Garsington Opera.
>
> Situated on high ground between the manor and village is St Mary's Church, built around 1200 and restored in 1849. From the churchyard there are extensive views to the Wittenham Clumps (see Walk 16). Near the door is a memorial to Lady Ottoline Morrell by Eric Gill.

Turn right along the lane passing an old granary store (raised on saddle-stones to discourage vermin), and later passing **Garsington Manor** and the village pond, known as the Gizzel. ◄ Follow the raised pavement up round the corner; **St Mary's Church**, with great views, is off to the left. At the split bear left – the **Three Horseshoes** can be seen on The Green – and at the next junction, with

The pond is fed by a spring, and the old English words *gysel* means 'gushing'.

The Manor House in Toot Baldon

the **Plough** ahead, turn right and then immediately keep left along **Oxford Road** for 200m.

④ **SU579025** After passing No. 27 **The Red Lion** can be seen ahead on the left; turn left along a path for 'Toot Baldon 1¾'. Cross the stile and continue along an enclosed path between the houses and then downhill, following a fence on the right for a while. At the hedge bear right, staying in the same field, and follow the hedge to the corner. Turn left crossing a footbridge and then right, now following the field edge and stream on the right. Keep ahead through the hedge gap in the field corner, cross the stile and turn left along the concrete track. Keep ahead over the road (B480), footbridge and stile to follow a path next to the hedge on the left; bear slightly right across the next field, aiming towards the electricity sub-station. Go through the hedge, cross the footbridge, and continue through the trees. At the far side cross a footbridge and follow the hedge on the right for 50m to a footpath post. Turn left across the field and continue through the hedge, later following a track into **Toot Baldon** and passing the **Manor House** to reach a T-junction.

> **Toot Baldon** is one of several hamlets sharing the name Baldon, as a local rhyme recalls:
>
> *Marsh Baldon, Toot Baldon, Baldon on the Green*
> *Little Baldon, Big Baldon, Baldon-in-between.*
>
> Toot Baldon was probably the earliest settlement, dating back to Anglo-Saxon times; Toot means a 'look-out point', and Baldon is a corruption of the Anglo-Saxon name meaning 'Bealda's Hill'. St Lawrence's Church, although modified, is a good example of an early 13th-century church. The first clear reference to a church in the Baldons (likely to be St Lawrence) is a Papal Bull of 1163; furthermore the Baldon 'feast' for both villages was close to St Lawrence's Day. The adjacent manor house dates from the early 17th century.

The path heading for Chiselhampton

⑤ **SU567007** Turn right, passing **The Mole Inn**, and at the entrance to the car park turn left along a metalled drive, later gravel track, to reach **St Lawrence's Church**. Follow the track round to the right; and at the junction with a lane turn left down a gravel bridleway with the house on the right; cross the footbridge and continue with the hedge on the right up the rise. Ignore the crossing footpath and later, at the junction with another bridleway, turn left along a farm track (footpath only), following it right and left between the farm buildings and continue down the track for 250m, (part of the **Shakespeare Way**).

At the hedge on the right turn half-right across the field passing a solitary oak tree; continue across the next field passing to the left of a sycamore tree. Cross a footbridge and follow the path up over the next field, passing to the right of a stand of oak trees, to the far side. Go through the hedge gap and follow the hedge on the left through three fields.

At the far side of the third field turn right for a few metres, and then left crossing a footbridge into the next field. Follow the path diagonally over the field to the bottom right corner; while crossing the field there are views of **St Katherine's Church** and **Chiselhampton House**.

The 15th-century bridge close to The Coach & Horses at **Chiselhampton** was once the only bridge over the River Thame between Wheatley and Dorchester, and it was over this that Prince Rupert rode to victory at the Battle of Chalgrove in 1643. St Katherine's Church can be reached by a short detour (800m round trip) along the B480 heading north (the key can be obtained from the Coach and Horses when open). The unaltered Georgian chapel, built in the 1760s, was loved by the poet John Betjeman. The church – which has a clock turret resembling those on stable blocks of the period – was built by Charles Peers, as was Chiselhampton House.

The Coach and Horses at Chiselhampton

Cross the footbridge and continue through the trees before turning right along a track. Turn left, following the road (B4105) towards **Chiselhampton**, and at the junction with **The Coach & Horses** ahead turn right along the B480, using the pavement on the left side of the road. Follow the road for 550m, crossing the **River Thame**, and shortly after the gentle left bend turn left through the trees at the footpath sign, cross the stile and head diagonally right over the field to cross a footbridge and stile. Bear right with the fence on the left, go through a gate and bear right to follow a path between the wall and stream towards **Stadhampton**. Turn left along a gravel track and bear right along School Lane, go left along the road (A329), passing **The Crown** pub to reach the junction of the A329 and B480.

WALK 20
Historic Ewelme and Swyncombe

Distance	13¾ miles (22.1km) or 7¼ miles (11.5km)
Time	6 hours or 3 hours
Grade	3
Map	OS Explorer 171/Landranger 174
Start/finish	Car park at the recreation ground in Ewelme (SU648912)
Public transport	Thames Travel buses to Wallingford
Refreshments	Ewelme – The Shepherd's Hut (01491 835661) – short walk through village; Upper Maidensgrove – Five Horseshoes (01491 641282)

The walk starts from the peaceful historic Oxfordshire village of Ewelme, nestling in the foothills of the southern Chiltern escarpment. Spend some time looking round; the school is claimed to have been in continuous use since 1437, while the church is the resting place of relatives of the great poet Geoffrey Chaucer. The walk heads out through the characteristic beech woods and rolling contours of the Chiltern Hills, passing through Pishill Bottom, before reaching the picturesque village of Russell's Water, whose village pond played a part in the film *Chitty Chitty Bang Bang*. From here you can call in at the Five Horseshoes at Upper Maidensgrove. Admire the views from the garden before tackling the return leg back to Ewelme, passing through the hamlets of Cookley Green and Swyncombe. The walk can be shortened by following the Ridgeway from North Farm to Swyncombe.

Ewelme is a peaceful village on the Chiltern escarpment, with old watercress beds and picturesque cottages. The church, almshouses and school all date from the 1430s, and were founded by the Duke and Duchess of Suffolk. The school is believed to be the oldest in the country in continuous use. St Mary's Church has a stunningly detailed effigy of Alice Chaucer, Duchess of Suffolk (d. 1475), as well as the

The Five Horseshoes at Upper Maidensgrove, the only pub on the route, is conveniently situated around the halfway point.

183

altar tomb of Thomas Chaucer (d. 1434), son of Geoffrey Chaucer, and his wife Matilda Burghersh (d. 1436), who inherited the Manor of Ewelme from her father. The manor later passed to the Crown and resulted in the building of a palace by Henry VII, later used by Henry VIII, and childhood home of Elizabeth I; only parts remain in the present Georgian manor house. The churchyard is also the resting place of *Three Men in a Boat* author Jerome K. Jerome (1859–1927).

① **SU648912** From the car park walk back towards the village along the lower, left-hand road. Shortly after passing the **school** and **almshouses** turn right up **Burrows Hill** and at the fork keep right next to **St Mary's** churchyard up to the road. Cross almost straight over

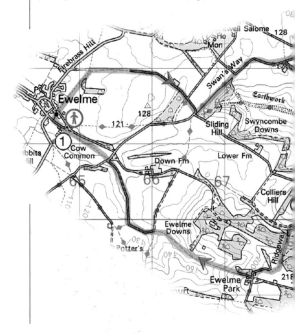

and at the driveway towards **Church Barn** take the path on the right-hand side of the drive, passing the church-yard extension on your right.

Continue with the fence on the right, ignoring a path to the left, and keep ahead across the field, before turning right along a gravel track. Keep ahead at the cross-tracks, then left up the left side of **Icknieldbank Plantation**, following **Swan's Way**. Keep to the main track as it bears to the right, to pass North Farm, now following the **Ridgeway**.

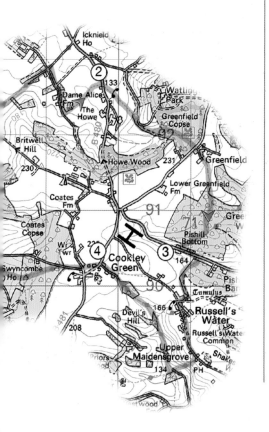

Shorter walk
At North Farm turn right along the Ridgeway to reach Swyncombe, where you can pick up the final section of the main walk.

Cross the lane – Britwell Hill Road – and keep along the Ridgeway/Swan's Way; further on there is a path for walkers on the right if the main track is muddy. At the cross-tracks junction, next to Lys Farm House, turn right to leave the Ridgeway and follow the bridleway passing **Dame Alice Farm**. After the trees turn left along the fenced path, to reach the road (B480) next to a house.

② **SU698926** Turn right for 50m and then left at the footpath sign; cross the stile into the field, following the right-hand fence. Cross the stile in the top corner and continue through the trees and a gate, bear left along the bridleway to pass another gate. At the Y-junction take the left-hand path up through **Greenfield Copse** (NT), ignoring any cross-tracks, to reach a gate leading to the road at Greenfield. Cross over and continue along the concrete track (bridleway); follow the track down across the field and enter **Greenfield Wood**. Bear right along the track at the Y-junction, up through the trees. At the T-junction, next to a pond, turn right along the track and down through the wood. Continue between the buildings at Grove Farm to pass a gate.

③ **SU708905** Turn left down the road (B480) through **Pishill Bottom** for just over 300m and then right at the gravel drive leading to Glade House. Where the drive turns right, take a sunken woodland path up ahead. Continue along the right-hand edge of **Russell's Water Common** and turn right along the lane between the houses. Walk past the picturesque village pond and then left along the road towards **Upper Maidensgrove** for 700m.

Upper Maidensgrove, with its sister hamlet – Maidensgrove – was known as Menygrove, 'common

The walk near Upper Maidensgrove: the Chilterns in autumn

clearing', in late medieval times. The village has the only pub on the route and the beer garden has a great view.

Just before the house turn right at the stile, signed 'Park Corner 1¼'. ▶ Follow the fenced path downhill, crossing three stiles, and then bear right to follow the hedge on the right steeply down into the valley. Cross the stile at the bottom and turn right along the bridleway going gently up the valley, and ignoring tracks to the left and right, to eventually pass some houses to reach the road (B481) at **Cookley Green**.

To visit **The Five Horseshoes** continue along the road for 100m, then return to this point.

Houses nestle round a large triangular green where a number of lanes converge. **Cookley Green** developed to house farm workers and servants from Swyncombe Park, where manor house, church, rectory and farm are situated.

187

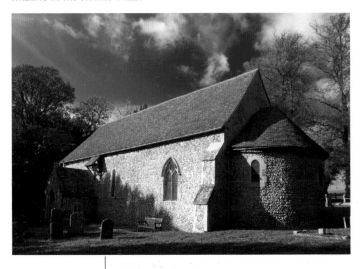

St Botolph's Church in
Swyncombe

④ **SU697903** Turn diagonally left over the road and follow a signed path across the village green (almost straight on). Keep ahead along Church Lane for 300m, ignoring the bridleway on the left; continue for a short distance further and cross the stile on the left to take the signed path half-left through **Church Wood**. Keep straight on at the path junction to reach a kissing gate at the far side of the wood. Walk down across **Swyncombe Park**, aiming slightly right of **Swyncombe House**, and go through the signed gate at the protruding corner of the fence. Follow the narrow enclosed path, cross the drive and continue through the trees. On reaching the large gate ahead turn right through the small gate and walk through **St Botolph's** churchyard, keeping to the left of the church, and go through the gate ahead.

The name **Swyncombe** is derived from the Old English *swin*, meaning 'wild boar' and *cumb*, 'valley'. After 1066 William the Conqueror delegated responsibility for his new kingdom to trusted officers and friends and, according to the Domesday Book, Milo Crispin was entrusted with Wallingford Castle which included the estate of Swyncombe. The Elizabethan manor house, Swyncombe House, once the home of Alice Chaucer (see notes on Ewelme), was extensively rebuilt around 1850. The Church of St Botolph is of early Norman origin.

⑤ **SU682902** Turn left along the lane and bear left down the track for 500m, now following the **Ridgeway**. Turn left, at the Ridgeway sign, through the trees and kissing gate, and up across the field to another kissing gate. Continue up through **Jacob's Tent** wood and then across the field following the left-hand fence. Bear right at the junction next to **Straights Plantation**, later bearing left to reach a cross-tracks at **Ewelme Park**.

Leave the Ridgeway and turn right down the track (bridleway) passing the stables. Shortly after the pond, keep straight on down to the left of the new plantation, following the hedge on the left side of the field, with views towards the **Wittenham Clumps**. Go through the gate and continue down a grassy track, with the fence on the right. At the junction with **Swan's Way** keep ahead gently uphill and at the Y-junction go right down the hedged bridleway, **Grindon Lane**. Cross straight over the road, go through the trees and kissing gate and continue across **Cow Common**, signposted 'Ewelme ½', to another couple of gates in the field corner leading back to the car park.

WALK 21

Roman around Silchester

Distance	11 miles (17.7km)
Time	4½ hours
Grade	1
Map	OS Explorer 159/Landranger 175
Start/finish	Mortimer railway station (SU672642); station car park (pay and display)
Public transport	Buses between Reading and Tadley stop at Mortimer
Refreshments	Stratfield Mortimer – Fox & Horn (0118 933 2428); Mortimer – local shops; Horse & Groom (0118 933 2813); Mortimer West End – Turners Arms (0118 933 2961); Padworth Common – The Round Oak (0118 970 0365)

This fairly easy walk, which starts from Mortimer railway station, leads through the gentle countryside straddling the Hampshire–Berkshire border and visits the remains of Calleva Atrebatum. Calleva is unusual in that – unlike many Roman towns such as Winchester and London which continued to prosper and grow after the Romans left – Calleva was completely abandoned. All that remains today are the impressive ruins of the town walls and the amphitheatre.

To find out more about the Roman town of Calleva Atrebatum you'll need to visit Reading Museum.

① **SU672642** From the railway station walk up to the road and go left along Station Road; just after the bridge over **Foudry Brook** turn right at the roundabout towards Reading. After 100m turn left opposite the telephone box, and follow the fenced gravel track, crossing Mortimer Lane and the V-stile leading into the field. Continue uphill, keeping close to the fence, later passing **Monkton Copse** on your left, and follow the farm track to pass through Wheat's Farm. At the cross-tracks bear half-left across the grassy bank to reach a stile and follow the narrow path; at the fence ahead, turn right over a stile

The Roman walls at Calleva Atrebatum

and continue, keeping the fence on your left, through the fields. At the corner, go first right then left at the stile, again keeping the fence on the left, later with a hedge and trees on the right. At the T-junction go left into the wood and shortly fork right at the post (yellow arrows). Cross over the road and through the gate opposite, next to the T-junction. Take the path diagonally across the recreation ground, known as 'The Fairground', aiming for the church to join Victoria Road in **Mortimer**. The **Horse & Groom** is to the left.

② **SU654646** Cross over and go along West End Road, passing the large Victorian **Church of St John the Evangelist**. Shortly after passing the post office and shops go left along St John's Road, then right along the gravel track between the houses. Keep straight on at the junction with **St Mary's Road** and turn right along **Drury Lane**, then left along **Turks Lane** for 100m. Turn right onto a narrow path between the houses, cross the stile and continue through the field with the hedge on the right; follow the path through the hedge into the next field, this time keeping the hedge on the left. At the field corner, cross the footbridge, and turn left along West End Road using the pavement on the right-hand side, passing the **Turners Arms**. Just after the last house on the left, about 400m along the road, cross over and turn left, following the track diagonally across the field aiming for the corner of the wood. Continue straight on downhill, with **Simm's Copse** on the left, turn right along the track, passing the power lines and bear left uphill, keeping straight on past **West End Farm**. At the lane, go right along the farm track (bridleway), later passing a playing field on the left. Turn right along Church Road to the T-junction.

③ **SU634642** Cross over and follow the path diagonally off to the left through the pine plantation. Go to the right along **Ramptons Lane** for 300m and turn left along the signposted path through the trees. Cross the footbridge and continue along the fenced path, bearing right along the track to reach the road at **Padworth Common**; the **Round Oak** is off to the right. Turn left for a short distance, then left

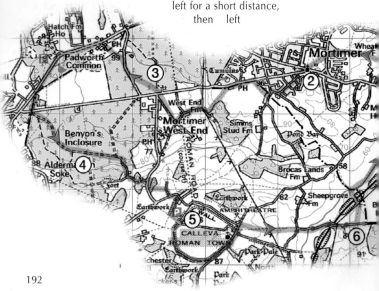

again onto the gravel drive of Manor House; immediately take the path off to the right through the trees to cross another gravel drive. Take the right-hand path at the fork (straight-on) across **Padworth Common**.

Turn left along the road and then left again along Chapel Lane, passing **West End Chapel**. At the T-junction cross straight over **Welshman's Road** and continue into **Benyon's Enclosure**. This plantation is part of the Englefield estate and the owners have allowed the public to walk along all the paths and rides; the next section of the walk follows one of these rides. Just after passing the power line keep to the main gravel track for just under ¾ mile (1.2km) to reach a main cross-tracks (SU624635). ▶

④ **SU624635** From the cross-tracks continue in an easterly direction, keeping to the main track; after 450m bear right and then left to reach the picturesque **Kiln Pond**. Cross between the ponds, and at the T-junction follow the track to the left. Continue up through the wood passing a house and small parking area. Turn right along the road, and at the start of the trees on the left turn left down an indistinct path; the sign is on the opposite side of the road. Go down through the trees and then up to reach a stile, cross over the field to another stile and then down a short track through the trees. Turn right along the gravel track (byway) up to the road, opposite the entrance to Mill Lane car park. Cross straight over and go through the car park keeping to the right-hand side; at the trees turn right along the path, with the remains of an ancient earthwork in the trees on the left. Follow the fenced path to the left and then right after passing a gate and, after a short distance, go left to reach the remains of the Roman town of **Calleva Atrebatum**.

Calleva Atrebatum, capital of the region formerly ruled by the late Iron Age Atrebates tribe, was an important

Note If the right of access is removed, walk along Welshman's Road for 700m and just after the electricity sub-station turn right, following the public footpath down to the cross-tracks at SU624635.

town in Roman Britain, standing at the junction of a number of major routes leading to other towns such as Winchester, Chichester, London, Dorchester (Dorset) and Salisbury. However, Calleva is almost unique in that, unlike comparable Roman towns, it never re-emerged in the later Anglo-Saxon period; the site was completely abandoned after the Romans departed. All that remains visible today are the amphitheatre and the defensive walls which stretch for 1½ miles (2.4km), reaching a height of 4m (13ft) in places.

Excavations within the walls – which were built around 200 years after the town was first occupied, shortly after the Roman invasion of AD43 – have shown that the town was laid out in a typical grid fashion, centred round the forum and adjoining basilica. These two buildings combined various functions, being both a market place and a seat of administration and justice. Other important buildings included temples, public bathhouses and an early Christian church.

⑤ **SU636625** Ignore the broad track ahead, but instead follow the track to the right, go through the gate and follow the path below the walls, later following the top of the wall. This eventually leads to a small gate into **St Mary's** churchyard.

The local church, St Mary the Virgin, at **Silchester** stands on the eastern side of the former Roman town, within the ruined walls and close to the amphitheatre, some distance from the present village. The church has undergone many alterations over the years, though many original features survive. The north doorway shows typical Norman 'dog-tooth' ornamentation and in the chancel is some original mid-13th century painted decoration. In the south aisle there is a 14th-century carved effigy of Eleanor Baynard, daughter of Sir John Bluet, the last male in the line of Bluets who had held the manor at Silchester since the Norman Conquest. The church

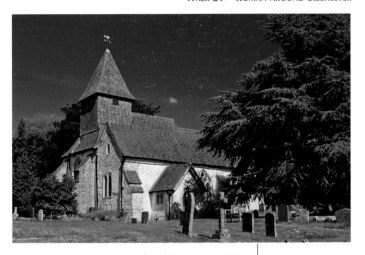

St Mary the Virgin Church, Silchester

screen, dating from the time of Henry VIII, is said to be one of the finest in Hampshire; the late 18th-century organ was first installed in St Paul's Church at Tottenham in London. The most recent addition is the wooden figure of Christ above the altar by the sculptor Peter Eugene Ball.

Follow the path to the right round the church and leave through the gate, passing a small pond. Turn left along the lane, ignoring the road off to the right and, at the sharp left-hand bend, make a short detour through the gate ahead to the remains of the Roman amphitheatre.

Located on the eastern edge of the Roman town (SU644626), the **Roman amphitheatre** was first built between AD50 and 70. Soil from the arena – the surface of which lies some 2m (6½ft) below ground level – was used to build the seating banks; the original timber wooden faces were replaced by stone walls during the 3rd century. During the 12th century a hall was built within the ruins, though there are no visible remains today. Some claim this to be a possible site of

Castellum de Silva, said to have been taken by King Stephen in 1147, during his war with Matilda.

However, the route turns right here, following a signed footpath through a gap in the hedge and down across the open field; now following the line of a former Roman road – The Devil's Highway – which connected Calleva Atrebatum with London. Continue under the power lines and at the far side of the field keep ahead along the lane, following it over the railway.

⑥ **SU661625** Just before the house on the right, **The Jackdaw**, turn left up the bank and through the gateway into the field. Follow the left-hand boundary, passing under the power lines and over the railway down to the field corner. Cross the stile and footbridge and then another stile, turn right and follow the right-hand field edge, passing a gate and footbridge on the way. At the field corner, with the trees ahead, go left for a short distance, cross the stile and turn right along the field edge. Where a path joins from the left, turn right across the footbridge and then left to follow the right-hand bank of the **Foudry Brook**. Follow the path as it bears right and then left round a pond, cross the bridge and go along the lane; **St Mary's Church** is on the left.

St Mary's Church at **Stratfield Mortimer** was built in 1869 over the foundations of a previous church and has some interesting features. The church is usually locked, though the key is available; see the sign in the lych-gate or call the parish office (0118 9333704). There is an octagonal font, possibly dating from the 12th century, and a stained-glass window composed in part of glass from the original Norman church. A rare inscribed Anglo-Saxon tomb slab was found under the old church tower, with the following inscription:

> On the 8th before the Kalends of October, Aegalward son of Kypping was laid in this place, Blessed be he who prays for his soul. Toki wrote this.

Aegalward, an influential historian and the first translator of the Anglo-Saxon Chronicle (AD994), was the son of Kypping, lord of the manor at Mortimer. Toki, who made the monument, was a wealthy courtier during the reign of King Canute (1017–35).

The Fox & Horn pub at Stratfield Mortimer

Turn right along the lane and then right at the road, following the pavement down past the **Fox & Horn**. At the roundabout go right, and then right again back to the railway station.

WALK 22

Chiltern Patchwork

Distance	14¼ miles (22.9km)
Time	6¾ hours
Grade	3
Map	OS Explorer 171/Landranger 175
Start/finish	Watlington Hill National Trust car park (SU710936)
Public transport	Buses between Wallingford and Henley-on-Thames stop at Nettlebed (1½ miles/2.4km away)
Refreshments	Ibstone – The Fox (01491 638289); Fingest – The Chequers Inn (01491 638335); Turville – Bull and Butcher (01491 638283); Pishill – The Crown Inn (01491 638364); Christmas Common – Fox & Hounds (01491 612599)

This walk weaves its way through a classic landscape of rounded chalk hills, a patchwork of beech woods and open farmland, in the southern Chilterns to the north of Henley-on-Thames. The walk starts at Christmas Common, said to be named after a short truce here on Christmas Day 1643 during the Civil War, and passes through Fingest with its unusual church tower and the picture-postcard village of Turville – known to many as the setting for the BBCtv comedy *The Vicar of Dibley*. The village is overlooked by Cobstone Windmill, which appeared in the film *Chitty Chitty Bang Bang*. From Turville the walk passes Stonor House, before climbing gently through the beech woods to arrive back at Watlington Hill.

Throughout this walk keep a look out for the impressive red kites that were reintroduced to the Chilterns in the early 1990s.

① **SU710936** From the car park go along Hill Road towards **Christmas Common** and turn left towards Stokenchurch. Just after passing the speed sign turn right along the first gravel drive, signed to **Magpie Cottage**. Where the drive bends to the right continue straight on along a narrow path into the trees, shortly bearing left. At the T-junction go right for 100m and then left at the

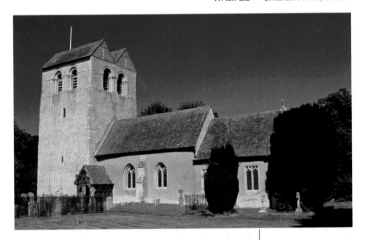

St Bartholomew's Church with its rare twin-gabled tower at Fingest

Y-junction down through the wood for about 1 mile (1.6km), following white arrows on trees. Keep to the right of the high wall, and at the lane go right for a few metres, then left through a gate and over the field. Cross the lane, two stiles, and over the field to cross two more stiles. At the junction with a bridleway continue straight on uphill, keeping close to the left-hand fence, and at the field corner follow the steep path into **Great Wood** and turn right along a bridleway. Bear left to reach the pond and then right to join the road opposite **The Fox** at Ibstone.

② **SU751939** Turn right and, after 500m, go left down the gravel track (footpath sign). Cross the field, close to the left-hand hedge, and continue down through the trees of **Twigside Bottom**. On reaching the junction at the bottom of the valley, turn right and follow the path along the wooded valley for 1½ miles (2.4km), later enclosed between fields, to reach **Chequers Lane**. Turn right towards the village of **Fingest**, passing **St Bartholomew's Church** on the right.

Fingest is a small village, once home to Sir William Connor (1909–67), who wrote for the *Daily Mirror* under the name of 'Cassandra', with an interesting

collection of picturesque cottages, church and the
Chequers Inn. St Bartholomew's Church (named after
one of the 12 apostles) has a very unusual twin-gabled
square Norman tower (there may only be one other
example in the country), and a painted plaster exterior
(most local churches have bare flint). The
village enjoys an

old wedding custom: to ensure good luck in marriage the bridegroom lifts his bride over the church gate after the ceremony.

At the T-junction, with **The Chequers Inn** ahead, turn right for 100m and then right through a gate at the end of the churchyard. Continue up along a narrow enclosed path, later passing through a wood. Go through the gate and cross over the lane to follow the path ahead, later crossing a stile. Follow the path diagonally down across the field towards **Turville**; on the hill to the right is **Cobstone Windmill**.

Cobstone Windmill (private) overlooks the village. This 18th-century smock mill had a revolving top section to allow the sails to be brought in line with the wind. The windmill – which appeared in an episode of the TV series *The New Avengers* in 1976 – played a starring role in the film *Chitty Chitty Bang Bang* (written by James Bond creator Ian Fleming) as the home of the eccentric inventor Caractacus Potts.

On reaching the field corner, go left down the gravel track between the houses to reach the main street; to the left is the timber-framed **Bull and Butcher**, while to the right is **St Mary's Church**.

Turville is a secluded picture-postcard village that has been used in many film and TV productions, including the BBC's *The Vicar of Dibley* and the ITV wartime drama *Goodnight Mister Tom*, and several episodes of *Midsomer Murders*. The village – Therfield, 'dry field', in Anglo-Saxon times – has a fine collection of 16th- to 18th-century cottages, as well as the picturesque timber-framed Bull and Butcher pub.

The 12th-century flint church of St Mary the Virgin boasts a few Norman features, though most of what you see is around 700 years old. A more recent addition is the vivid blue stained-glass window by John Piper – who designed the magnificent stained glass for Coventry Cathedral – which commemorates St Saviour's church in nearby Turville Heath, which closed in 1972. There is an ornate marble monument to the lord of the manor, William Perry, great grandfather of the poet Percy Bysshe Shelley. During restoration work in 1901 an old stone coffin was found

Cobstone Windmill at Turville

Chiltern scenery at Turville

beneath the floor, containing two burials, one from around 700 years ago and a 16th-century skeleton of a woman with a hole in her skull.

③ **SU769901** Cross diagonally right, keeping left of the small green, to take the lane up between the cottages. Keep ahead with the field boundary on the right, cross over the lane near **Dolesden Farm** and continue uphill to a stile. Go through the wood to another stile and then over the middle of the field to a stile at **Southend Farm**. Follow the concrete track to the road, turn left for 150m and, just after the cottage, turn right towards **Stonor Park**. Follow the track down through the trees for 500m and at the Y-junction take the left-hand track through **Kildridge Wood** to a kissing gate. Follow the waymarked (white arrows) path across the deer parkland, following the fence on the left; later on **Stonor House** can be seen to the right. Go through the kissing gate at the lower left corner of the parkland.

Stonor House and park

Stonor House has been the home of Lord and Lady Camoys and the Stonor family for over 800 years. The house, hidden in a fold of the Chilterns and surrounded by a deer park, started life in the late 1100s. By 1540 it had taken on a classic 'E' shape, with a later Georgian brick façade built over the original timber and flint structure. The Stonor family refused to renounce Catholicism and as a result Stonor became a refuge for Catholics, among them the Jesuit scholar and missionary Edmund Campion, executed in 1581 and later canonised. During this time the Stonor family were imprisoned and deprived of their land, though later reinstated, and their descendants still live here (opening times: 01491 638587).

④ **SU737889** Turn right along the road (B480) for 800m and, shortly after the turning for Turville Heath, turn left between the hedges up to the woodland. Continue up through the trees for 750m to meet a track near to **Maidensgrove** village. Turn sharp right, now following the **Oxfordshire Way**, and walk down through **Pishillbury Wood**; after the cross-tracks follow the right-hand field boundary, keeping straight on at the fork in the track. Follow the fenced track next to the garden and along the lane down past **Pishill Church** to join the road (B480); **The Crown Inn** is a short distance to the left.

> The small hamlet of **Pishill** consists of a church, pub and a few houses. The church dates back to Norman times, though it was partially rebuilt in 1854. There are several interesting stained-glass windows, including one in memory of Philip Hall, the lay reader for many years; the 6th Lord Camoys commissioned John Piper, who lived at Fawley, to create the window. It shows St Paul's emblems, the Sword and Gospel; the Gospel held by two hands in front of the Sword, signifying that the pen is mightier than the sword.

⑤ **SU727900** Turn right for 50m, then left on a track past **Pishill Farm**; the route back to **Christmas Common** follows the **Oxfordshire Way** (OW signs on trees). Continue up the valley and after entering College Wood leave the track, and bear slightly right up through the trees, looking out for OW signs. After 800m cross a stile, leave the wood, and over the field to a stile. Cross **Hollandridge Lane** and go straight on, passing two ponds on the right, to a stile at the wood. Continue for 100m to a cross-tracks and take the left-hand track up through **Fire Wood**. Later the track bears left and joins Hollandridge Lane; turn right up the lane for 100m and just after the house on the left, turn left onto a gravel driveway. Next to the garage, turn half-right (OW sign on tree) through the wood, passing just to the right of the old church and churchyard. Turn right along the road, passing the **Fox and Hounds**, and at the junction go left back to the car park.

WALK 23

Thames and Chilterns Meander

Distance	15 miles (24.1km)
Time	6¼ hours
Grade	2
Map	OS Explorer 171/Landranger 175
Start/finish	Limited roadside parking in High Street off B478, Sonning (SU757755) – see below for alternative options
Public transport	Trains to Shiplake, buses from High Wycombe, Marlow, Wokingham and Reading stop at either Sonning or Shiplake
Refreshments	Sonning – Bull Inn (0118 969 3901); Play Hatch – Flowing Spring (0118 969 3207); Binfield Heath – Bottle & Glass (01491 575755); Lower Shiplake – Baskerville Arms (0118 940 3332)

This meandering walk leads through typical Chiltern countryside before following the peaceful banks of the River Thames, with plenty of opportunities for seeing varied wildlife, including red kites and kingfishers. The walk starts at Sonning and passes through several hamlets as well as Crowsley Park, once home to the Baskerville family, friends of Sir Arthur Conan Doyle. The route then heads for Binfield Heath, before descending along the edge of Henley-on-Thames, and finally following the Thames Path back to Sonning. On the way you can make a short detour to Shiplake church where the poet Alfred Lord Tennyson married Emily Sellwood.

The route starts from Sonning but you can also start from Mill Lane car park in Henley-on-Thames or Shiplake railway station.

Sonning – the name is thought to derive from that of a Saxon chief, Sunna – is situated on the banks of the River Thames and was described by Jerome K. Jerome in *Three Men in a Boat* as 'the most fairy-like little nook on the whole river'. St Andrew's Church dates from the 1100s, though was heavily restored in the 19th century, and has some impressive monuments

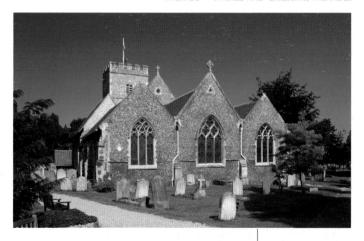

St Andrew's Church at Sonning

and brasses; the Bull Inn, next to the church, is thought to have been the Bishops' Guesthouse. The elegant red-brick multi-arched bridge over the Thames was built in 1775 and links Sonning in Berkshire with Sonning Eye in Oxfordshire. A stone marker at the centre is marked 'B | O', the vertical line indicating the mid-river boundary. Located on an island between the two bridges is Sonning Mill, an old flour mill that has been converted into a 'dinner theatre'.

① **SU757755** Walk down the High Street and turn right past the **Bull Inn** and through the churchyard passing to the left of **St Andrew's Church**, to leave along a fenced path. Turn right along the riverbank, and then left to cross two bridges over the Thames and passing The Mill at Sonning theatre. After crossing the second bridge, with the **French Horn** on the right, bear half-left at the car park, then right at Furleigh Cottages, following the narrow enclosed metalled path through **Sonning Eye**. Turn left along the lane, following it round to the right, go through the gate ahead and cross over the B478 to continue along **Spring Lane**.

After 150m go right over a stile into the field and follow the hedge on the left through two fields, parallel to the lane. Cross the stile on the left and continue along the lane to a junction with the A4155, next to the **Flowing Spring**. Cross

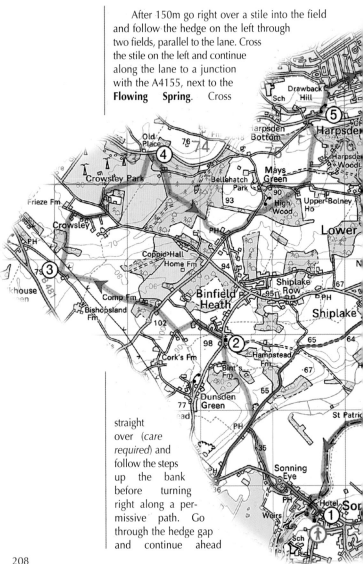

straight over (*care required*) and follow the steps up the bank before turning right along a permissive path. Go through the hedge gap and continue ahead

208

before bearing left uphill (bridle-way). At the junction with a path keep straight on and turn right along the road towards **Binfield Heath**, passing the small mock-gothic **Congregational Chapel** built in 1835.

② **SU743779** At the junction turn left along **Gravel Road** for 470m. After the last house and the speed sign, turn left along a path for 'Sandpit Lane'. Follow the left-hand hedge and then bear right along a gravel track – **Sandpit Lane** – for a few metres, turn right over a footbridge and stile in the hedge. Keep ahead over the field passing the stand of trees, later following a hedge on the left. At the large oak tree bear half-right across the field, to follow the hedge on the left. Cross straight over the road and follow the gravel track ahead. Shortly after passing some barns and a house on the right, the track reaches open fields. Keep to the left-hand field, following the hedge on the right and continue through the hedge gap. At the next field corner, bear left and right (straight on), following the hedge on the right and pass under the power lines. At the field corner continue along a gravel track past the houses.

③ **SU721788** Turn right along the road for 75m and then right through the hedge to follow the path signposted 'Crowsley ¾', across the field, passing under the power lines. Cross the stile and continue down through the trees, bearing left along the track and then almost immediately right along a narrow path through the trees; look out for the white arrow on the tree, to reach an open field. Follow the left-hand boundary uphill, keeping **Morgan's Wood** on the left. Where the wood ends, follow the narrow enclosed path ahead. At the junction with another path, next to the gate on the left, keep straight on, now following part of the **Chiltern Way**, past some houses and turn right along the lane. Turn left along the road for 150m and right into the entrance to **Crowsley Park**, using the narrow gate on the right.

Now owned by the BBC, **Crowsley Park** was once the home of Henry Baskerville, who bought the estate in 1822. Family friend Sir Arthur Conan Doyle is thought to have based *The Hound of the Baskervilles* on the family and its estate. The story, set on Dartmoor (supposedly to protect the family's privacy), describes many characteristics of Crowsley Park. The Baskerville family coat of arms is based on a hound's head, and the entrance gateposts are still topped by two hound's heads with spears in their mouths.

Follow the metalled drive ahead and just after the second turning on the right, turn half-right through a gate and follow the fenced path to go through another gate. Continue over the field to cross a stile and keep ahead through the next field for 250m; to the left can be seen several large satellite receiving dishes. At the path junction (marker post), turn left, following a footpath downhill to a gate in the bottom right corner of the field.

④ **SU733804** After going through the gate, almost immediately turn sharp right to follow a signed bridleway 'Binfield Heath 1½', up through the trees. Cross over the track at **North Lodge** and follow the path down along the edge of the wood with a fence on the right, later bearing left down through the trees. Continue up through the trees, looking out for the blue/white arrows on the trees. At the top of the wood follow the bridleway to the right – Bones Lane – to reach a junction next to the

One of the hound's head gateposts at the entrance to Crowsley Park

Bottle & Glass. Turn left towards Harpsden and Henley-on-Thames for 500m and, at the bridleway sign, go diagonally right through **High Wood** to reach a lane.

Turn right (bridleway) and then cross the stile on the left to follow a footpath through the field, following the right-hand boundary. At the field corner don't cross the stile ahead, but instead turn left staying in the same field, following the fence on the right to cross a stile in the far corner. Continue straight on through two fields, following the fence on the right, and cross another stile to reach the golf course. Keep ahead, following the posts down the hill, and at the bottom turn left along the track (yellow arrow on post). At the road turn right and right at the junction, following the road through **Harpsden** for 150m.

⑤ **SU756809** After the last house on the left and before the playing field, turn left along a fenced path, signed 'Henley 1'. Cross the stile and continue steeply uphill to cross another stile before following the narrow fenced path, keeping ahead at the driveway – **Rotherfield Road**. Bear right down the lane on the outskirts of **Henley-on-Thames**, passing several streets on the left. At the T-junction with Harpsden Way continue straight on following the fenced track (bridleway) down between the houses, later a road, to reach the A4155.

Cross slightly to the right to follow **Mill Lane**, passing over the railway line before going past Mill Lane car park on the left (*alternative start point*).

Bear right along the **Thames Path**, following the wooden walkways past **Marsh Lock**. Continue along the riverside path towards **Lower Shiplake**, later bearing right away from the river. Cross a footbridge and continue along a fenced path next to a private drive, later following Bolney Road. Bear diagonally right at the Thames Path sign along a narrow fenced path and turn left just before the railway line for 100m, turn right at the road to cross the railway track, passing **Shiplake Station**.

George Orwell (1903–50), author of such classics as *Animal Farm* and *1984*, lived with his parents for several years in **Lower Shiplake**, close to the railway station. Orwell, born Eric Arthur Blair – he only started using the pseudonym 'George Orwell' in 1933 – had his first work, *Awake Young Men of England*, published in 1914 while living in the village.

⑥ **SU775797** Continue along the road and at the junction, next to the **Baskerville Arms**, turn left for 700m before going left at the Thames Path sign towards **Lashbrook Farm**. Just after crossing the bridge, turn right down to a kissing gate, signed 'Thames Path & Shiplake Lock ¼'; follow the path across the narrow field to go through another kissing gate. Bear slightly right to follow the field boundary on the right, keep ahead over the farm track and along the fenced path. Turn right along **Mill Lane** for a few metres and then left, signposted 'Thames Path & Sonning 3', turning right along the riverside path. On reaching **Shiplake College Boathouse** you can make a short detour up to the church.

Detour
Just before the bridge turn right along a signed bridleway following the hedge for a few metres, then bear

A peaceful scene on the River Thames near Shiplake College

left passing between the clubhouse and boathouse, heading away from the river. Follow the path as it turns sharp right uphill to reach the **Church of St Peter and Paul**. Retrace the route back to the bridge.

Parts of the **Parish Church of St Peter and St Paul** in **Shiplake**, including the tower, date from around 1140, while the Jacobean pulpit came from All Saints Church in Dorchester (Dorset), and the impressive French medieval glass came from the ruined Abbey of St Bertin at St Omer. Alfred Lord Tennyson (1809–92) married Emily Sellwood here in 1850. Next to the church is Shiplake Court, built in the 1890s on the site of a much older house; it was used by the BBC during World War II, becoming a school (Shiplake College) in 1959.

To continue the walk keep along the **Thames Path** to **Sonning**, crossing the footbridge and going left along the B478 over the Thames. Continue past the **Great House Hotel** and up Thames Street, keeping to the pavement on the left; at the top of the rise turn right down the High Street.

213

WALK 24
Hambleden Valley and a Royal Regatta

Distance	13½ miles (21.7km)
Time	5½ hours
Grade	1
Map	OS Explorer 171/Landranger 175
Start/finish	Henley-on-Thames railway station; nearby pay and display car park at Mill Meadows (SU765822)
Public transport	Trains to Henley-on-Thames, and bus links to Wallingford
Refreshments	Henley-on-Thames – pubs and shops; Hambleden – Stag & Huntsman (01491 571227); Medmenham – Dog & Badger (01491 571362); Aston – Flowerpot Inn (01491 574721)

Henley-on-Thames, on the banks of the River Thames, has been synonymous with rowing since 1829 when crews from Oxford and Cambridge universities held their first race here; in 1851 the Henley Royal Regatta became an important annual event. However, our reasons for visiting Henley-on-Thames have little to do with boats, but more with the fact that the town lies on the edge of the beautiful Chiltern Hills. This figure-of-eight route leads along the peaceful river before heading along the Hambleden Valley, with its typical Chiltern scenery. The return leg passes through the villages of Medmenham and Aston before arriving back at Henley.

Henley-on-Thames is best known for its famous Royal Regatta, held in July, when the river is swamped with boats and rowers.

The prosperous and historic market town of **Henley-on-Thames** was once described by Charles Dickens as 'the Mecca of the rowing man', and Henley-on-Thames has been inextricably linked with the sport since 1829. Within 10 years the first regatta was held and in 1851, when HRH Prince Albert became the first royal patron, the event became known as the Henley Royal Regatta. The Leander Club, claimed to be the

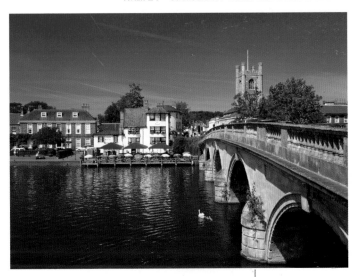

The River Thames at Henley-on-Thames

world's oldest rowing club (founded in London in 1818) has been based in Henley-on-Thames since 1896; famous members include the Olympic rowers Sir Steven Redgrave and Matthew Pinsent. The town is also home to the award-winning River and Rowing Museum, opened in 1998 and near the start of the walk (01491 415600).

St Mary's Parish Church dates from the early 1200s, although was rebuilt on a grander scale during the 15th century, and has some good Victorian stained-glass windows. The five-arched bridge over the Thames was built in 1787 to replace an earlier wooden one; the two carved heads on the central arch represent Isis and Old Father Thames.

① **SU765822** Walk northwards up to Station Road and bear right along Thames Side, with the **River Thames** on the right, to reach Hart Street (A4130); **St Mary's Church** and the **Red Lion Hotel** are ahead, and the **Market Place** to the left. Turn right, past **The Angel on the Bridge** and over the river before going left, following the **Thames Path**. Bear right past the **Leander Club**, and later passing **Remenham**; this stretch of river, the longest reach on the Thames, is used for the Royal Regatta, with races starting from **Temple Island**.

The walk just passes to the west of the little hamlet of **Remenham**. In the trees can be seen the flint tower of St Nicholas' Church

(usually locked).
Along the Thames Path here you'll pass Temple Island with a folly built in 1771 by James Wyatt, as both a summerhouse/fishing lodge and to improve the vista from Fawley Court, situated on the far side of the river and built by Sir Christopher Wren in 1684. The island marks the start of the regatta course, set

at 1 mile 550yds. Further along the river is Greenlands, now Henley Management College; the original house was destroyed by Cromwellian forces during the Civil War in 1644. The present Italianate mansion was once owned by the newspaper magnate W.H. Smith, Viscount Hambleden.

At **Hambleden Lock** cross the river via the lock and weirs to reach the picturesque white weatherboarded **Hambleden Mill** (private), much loved by photographers and painters alike. Follow the fenced path round the mill to join the road (A4155) at **Mill End**, turn right for a few metres before crossing over (*care required*) and following the road for Hambleden, Skirmett and Fingest.

② **SU786854** At the next junction, to Rotten Row, leave the road and go through the kissing gate ahead, following the path across the field, parallel to the road. Keep ahead through two gates either side of a farm track towards **Hambleden**, aiming for the church.

The picturesque village of **Hambleden** with 400-year-old cottages clustered round the church has seen its fair share of film action, including Walt Disney's *101 Dalmatians*, *The New Avengers* and *Sleepy Hollow*, along with TV appearances in programmes such as of *Midsomer Murders*. Running through the village is the Hamble Brook, a typical chalk stream fed from groundwater stored within an aquifer (a layer of chalk that acts like a sponge). The upper reaches of the brook are termed as a 'winterbourne', a stream that usually only flows during very wet winter months.

St Mary's Church dates back 800 years, and has a 12th-century carved font and a 16th-century oak altar, the Wolsey Altar; the wood panelling bears the coat of arms of Cardinal Wolsey, and is claimed to have come from his bedstead. The manor house dates from 1604 and was the birthplace of James Thomas Brudenell (1797–1868), 7th Earl of Cardigan (later Lord Cardigan), who led the famous Charge of the Light Brigade at Balaclava during the Crimean War (1854). Another famous son of the village was St Thomas de Cantilupe (1218–82), the last Englishman to be canonised before the Reformation, also Bishop of Hereford and an advisor to Edward I. In the churchyard is the grave of Victorian bookseller and government minister W.H. Smith, the 1st Viscount Hambleden (1825–91); the first William Henry Smith (1792–1865) lent his name to the family empire, which started out as a small newsagent's shop on The Strand, London.

Turn right at the road over **Hambleden Brook** (often dry) and continue through the village, passing the shop and bearing right in front of the lych-gate leading to **St Mary's Church**. Continue along the lane past the **Stag & Huntsman** and up the hill, turning right just before the buildings, along a farm track. After passing the last house turn left up a narrow enclosed path; before entering the wood stop and admire the view across the valley. On the far side of the wood, walk across the field and straight on at the cross-tracks to join a lane bearing left. Where the lane turns to the left, keep ahead through the gate and across the field. In the next field follow the left-hand fence to reach a stile in the far corner, go through the trees and then right along the lane for 500m.

③ **SU809865** At the house on the left, close to the bend in the road, turn right through the hedge to a concealed gate and footpath sign. Follow the left-hand field edge to a stile and then right passing **Bockmer House**. Just after the pond, leave the drive and follow the path to

the right through the field, keeping parallel to the pylons. After passing through the belt of trees bear slightly left to reach a stile and gate in some trees on the left side of the field and join **Bockmer Lane**. Turn right down to the crossroads at **Medmenham**; on the right is the **Dog & Badger**.

Hambleden Mill on the River Thames

Medmenham is strung out along Ferry Lane down to the river. The Norman St Peter and St Paul Church dates from around 1200, though was heavily restored in the 19th century. Medmenham Abbey was founded in the 12th century. Little remains of the original Cistercian abbey which was destroyed during the reign of Henry VIII; the present so-called abbey is a house dating from 1595. The 'ecclesiastical' remains are follies built by one-time Chancellor of the Exchequer Sir Francis Dashwood (1708–81) in the 1750s. Dashwood used the house as the meeting place for the Medmenham Club, who originally called themselves 'The Franciscans' or 'Medmenham Monks' and included many leading figures of the time. Their infamous reputation and well-known nickname 'The Hell Fire Club'

219

came later, and eventually the group was disbanded as stories of lewd acts became widespread.

Cross over the A4155 and down **Ferry Lane**, passing the **Church of St Peter and St Paul**, and turn right along the Thames. In the trees is a monument commemorating the 1899 Court of Appeal ruling that the Medmenham ferry, which used to cross the river here, was public owned.

④ **SU806837** Continue along the riverbank, and at the hedge across the path turn right then left along a lane to join the A4155. Follow the road towards **Mill End** for a short way and then left along the footpath past the mill building and back across the weirs at **Hambleden Lock**. On the far side of the river turn left along the **Thames Path**, keeping left at the split following the riverbank. Turn right up the lane to the T-junction, next to the **Flowerpot Inn**.

⑤ **SU784842** Turn right along **Remenham Lane** for about 160m and, after the last house turn left up the track (permissive path), keeping close to the left-hand boundary. At the top of the hill, turn right along the track. ◄ Follow the track ahead, with good views of the Chilterns on the right, and cross the stile next to the gate. Bear left along the lane for 220m and turn right at the footpath sign through the hedge and across the field.

Descend to **Remenham Wood** and follow the path up through the trees. Cross the stile at the far side and continue diagonally right over the field to join another path, bearing left just inside the wood down to a stile. Go across the open ground to another stile near the far right corner, and then straight over the grassy field to a gate and **Remenham Lane**.

Here, you can either go left along the lane to reach the A423 or cross straight over and go through the gap in the hedge, bearing left at the track to reach the A423. Follow the road to the right, crossing the river, and turn left along **Thames Side** back to the car park.

Note If the right of access is removed, continue straight on up Aston Lane and immediately after the last house turn right along a narrow signposted path, cross the stile and follow the path uphill, keeping to the right-hand side of the field to join a track.

WALK 25

Cookham and Stanley Spencer

Distance	14½ miles (23.3km) or 9 miles (14.5km)
Time	6 hours or 3¾ hours
Grade	1
Map	OS Explorer 172/Landranger 175
Start/finish	Cookham Moor National Trust car park (SU892853)
Public transport	Trains to Cookham and Bourne End, buses from Maidenhead to Cookham
Refreshments	Cookham Dean – Jolly Farmer (01628 482905); Marlow – pubs, shops and restaurants; Cookham – pubs, shops and restaurants; Boulter's Lock Island – café

The walk starts at Cookham Moor (National Trust) and passes through Cookham Rise and Cookham Dean before descending through Bisham Wood to cross the River Thames at Marlow with its famous suspension bridge. The next section follows the Thames Path for several miles to Boulter's Lock. This is a particularly picturesque stretch of the River Thames, including beautiful Cliveden Reach, perfectly captured by Jerome K. Jerome (1859–1927) in *Three Men in a Boat*: 'In its unbroken loveliness this is, perhaps, the sweetest stretch of all the river.' On the way the route passes through Cookham, the home of artist Sir Stanley Spencer. From Boulter's Lock, on the northern edge of Maidenhead, the final leg heads across Widbrook Common with its views towards Cliveden House, then back to Cookham Moor.

① **SU892853** Cross over the road and follow the raised walkway to the right over the old bridge, later following the pavement along the road, passing **Spencers** and the **Old Swan Uppers**. At the junction go straight on towards **Cookham Dean** and station (alternative start point) passing through **Cookham Rise**. Cross over the railway track and immediately turn left along **High Road**, following it round to the right. At the junction

A fairly long walk, although mostly over level ground; it can be shortened by missing out the final section from Cookham to Boulter's Lock.

with Worcester Road, just after a school, is the house (Cliveden View) where Sir Stanley Spencer lived from 1944 to 1958 (blue plaque).

Famous inhabitants of **Cookham Rise and Cookham Dean** have not only included Sir Stanley Spencer (see section on Cookham), but also Kenneth Grahame (1859–1932) author of *The Wind in the Willows*, who spent his early childhood living with his grandmother at The Mount (now Herries School) in Dean Lane, and Guglielmo Marconi (1874–1937), pioneer of wireless communication, who lived at Hillyers in Whyteladies Lane (No. 142).

The Church of St John the Baptist in Cookham Dean dates from the 1840s, and has some good examples of Victorian stained glass. One unusual feature is that there are two lych-gates, where coffins were rested briefly for the first part of the burial service; *lych* is Anglo-Saxon for 'corpse'.

Continue along High Road and at the T-junction cross over **Whyteladies Lane** (Dean Lane is off to the right) slightly to the right to follow a signed path between the house and cricket ground. Continue along the enclosed path and keep to the left side of the field to follow a hedge-lined path uphill towards **Cookham Dean**, passing through a gate and later following a metalled lane past **St John the Baptist Church**. At the green turn right along the gravel track with the **Jolly Farmer** ahead and then right again, downhill with the church on the right.

② **SU872853** At the junction, next to the war memo-rial and **Cookham Dean Common** (NT), turn left. Follow the gravel track round to the left and then past the front of the **Inn on the Green**, keep ahead along a narrow path between the pub and house, later through the wood to a V-stile. Continue down the field and keep ahead at the path junction uphill with the

hedge on the right to reach a kissing gate. Turn left along the road for a short distance and then right, just before the house. Follow a signed bridleway through the trees of **Bisham Wood** (owned by the Woodland Trust), ignoring a path on the right and left. Follow a sunken track steeply downhill; where the track bends to the left, turn sharp right up a permissive bridleway (marked as a path on maps), and keep ahead following the line of blue-topped posts for about 700m. ◄

Where the bridleway bends to the right, take a rather overgrown path on the left through the scrub (look for yellow arrows on posts). Bear left down some steps and turn right up along the road (*care required*) for about 20m to go through a gap in the barrier on the left side of the road. Take the left-hand path down the steps, later bearing left and right to reach a road; continue ahead over the bridge and later under the A404 towards Bisham. At the junction go right to pass the **Compleat Angler Hotel** ◄ and cross over the **River Thames** at **Marlow** with the **All Saints Church** ahead.

Once a Saxon market town, **Marlow** has always been prosperous and during the 18th and 19th centuries became a fashionable place to live. Famous inhabitants have included the poet Percy Bysshe Shelley (1792–1822), who lived at Albion House in West Street and his wife Mary (1797–1851), who wrote *Frankenstein* while living in the town; a century later T.S. Eliot (1888–1965) lived in the same street. There's been a bridge across the Thames at Marlow since 1220s, although the present suspension bridge was built around 1830 by William Tierney Clark. Clark designed three other suspension bridges: Hammersmith, Shoreham and, the largest and most famous, the Széchenyi Bridge over the River Danube, linking the Hungarian towns of Buda and Pest.

All Saints Church was built in 1835, replacing the earlier 12th-century building, though records show that a church existed here in 1070. Some monuments have survived from the original church, and there are

To the left through the trees are views of Marlow and the River Thames.

The hotel was named after Izaak Walton's book *The Compleat Angler* which he wrote in 1653 while in Marlow.

The famous suspension bridge across the River Thames at Marlow

also 13 hatchments (a corruption of 'achievements'), the oldest of which is that of Sir William Clayton, 1st Baronet (d. 1744).

③ **SU851861** Shortly, turn right along the Thames Path through the churchyard and along the enclosed path, cross over St Peter's Street and keep ahead along the path, Seven Corners Alley, just right of the **Two Brewers**. Turn right along Mill Road, passing a path to Marlow weir and lock. Shortly after turn right along a path signed 'Thames Path – Bourne End 2' across the small grassy area, and then follow the riverside path to the railway bridge at **Bourne End**.

④ **SU892871** Cross over the bridge and turn left along the riverside path towards **Cookham**. Shortly before the bridge, bear half-right keeping to the **Thames Path** to pass through **Holy Trinity** churchyard, keeping to the left-hand path at the split to leave the churchyard via a gate.

Holy Trinity Church at **Cookham** dates from the 12th century, replacing an earlier Saxon structure, and has several interesting brasses and a copy Sir Stanley Spencer's *Last Supper*.

The famous English painter Sir Stanley Spencer (1891–1959), who lived in Cookham for most of his life, was born in a house called Fernlea along the High Street. The gallery (see below) – which opened in 1962 (unique in being the only one in Britain devoted exclusively to an artist in the village where he was born and spent most of his working life) – is located in the former Wesleyan chapel where Spencer worshipped as a child. One of his most famous works – *The Resurrection, Cookham* painted in 1926 – was set in the churchyard here. More of Stanley's work can be seen at the Sandham Memorial Chapel at Burghclere (Hampshire).

Follow the road and turn right along the road (A4094). On the opposite side is the **Tarry Stone**; this sarsen boulder set in the pavement has been mentioned in many historical documents, and a wall plaque claims it had something to do with village sports before 1507. Continue to the junction with the **Spencer Gallery** ahead.

Shorter walk
Turn right at the junction, following the High Street through the town, later following a traffic-free lane on the left of the road over Cookham Moor (NT) to reach the car park on the right.

To continue on the main walk keep ahead along Sutton Road (A4094) towards Maidenhead for 100m and then left along Mill Lane. Shortly before the end of the lane and just after the entrance to **The Drey** (private house) turn right keeping along the Thames Path, later staying parallel to a metalled lane, before bearing half-right along an enclosed path to reach the river. ◄

It was from here that the *My Lady* ferry ran until 1956.

Across the river at **Cliveden** and **Cliveden Reach** is the picturesque Spring Cottage built in 1813 and enlarged

Spring Cottage and the River Thames near Cookham

in the 1870s for the Duchess of Sutherland, lady-in-waiting and confidante of Queen Victoria. Above stands the Italianate mansion Cliveden House (best viewed from Widbrook Common), used as Lady Penelope's home in the recent *Thunderbirds* film. The house, designed by Sir Charles Barry (who also designed the Houses of Parliament), was built for the Duke of Sutherland. Cliveden will be forever linked with the Profumo affair; it was here that John Profumo, Secretary of State for War in the early 1960s, met Christine Keeler.

Turn right – on the opposite bank is **Spring Cottage –** passing **Cliveden Reach** and later following the road (A4094) to reach **Boulter's Lock** and the bridge to **Ray Mill Island**.

Boulter's Lock lock takes its name from the old English *bolter*, 'miller'; a mill was built on **Ray Mill Island** in 1726. The famous BBC broadcaster Richard Dimbleby

(1913–1965) lived on the northern tip of the island in the grey weathered-boarded visible from the Thames Path. Access to the island and café is by the bridge at the lock.

⑤ **SU903824** Turn right along **Ray Mill Road East**, and just after passing a road called The Pagoda, turn half-right along an enclosed path. Cross over **Sheephouse Road**, and continue ahead along **Summerleaze Road**. At the sharp left bend continue ahead along a signed footpath for a few metres and then go right along a gravel track, staying parallel with a lane on the right. Go through the hedge and follow the path to the left; at the metalled track turn sharp right over the bridge and then left through the gate to follow the **Green Way** over the grassy area. Go through the gap in the hedge and turn half-right over the field to continue north along the gravel track.

At the junction turn right along a track, keeping the gravel workings on the right. Just before a gate, turn left following a signed path over the field, cross the stile and footbridge over the **White Brook**, and keep ahead over **Widbrook Common** (NT), following the left-hand boundary. Turn left through a kissing gate and over the field; at the trees ignore the path ahead, but turn right staying in the same field and follow the **Green Way East**, with the trees and **Stand Water** on the left. Continue through the next field, keeping to the left-hand edge, and after crossing a track bear half-right to continue along the edge of the field. Bear left along an enclosed path to later reach a metalled drive with **Moor Hall** on the left (Chartered Institute of Marketing); the **Crown** can be seen ahead. Cross the drive and follow the path half-left across the grass and over the metalled path to reach the car park.

APPENDIX 1
A Brief History

Prehistoric Times

The region was probably first inhabited during the Palaeolithic or Old Stone Age, up to 10,500 years ago, when diverse habitats supported a wide range of animals and vegetation for the hunter-gatherer population. About 6000 years ago Neolithic farmers arrived and started to alter the landscape by cutting down trees to clear areas for planting and to provide grazing. Later the introduction of metal tools and weapons, initially bronze and progressing to iron, enabled more land to be cleared and lead to the development of cultivated, fortified settlements. All these peoples have left behind their mark on the countryside, from Neolithic long barrows such as Wayland's Smithy to Iron Age hillforts like Uffington and Segsbury on the Ridgeway, and Walbury Camp. It was during this time – around 4000BC – that man first started walking the Ridgeway, one of the oldest green roads in England. The tracks provided a safer high-level route above densely forested lower ground, and was also drier in the winter months. However, perhaps the most remarkable feature dating from antiquity is the Uffington White Horse, originally made during the Bronze Age. Its image was later used on coins of the Atrebates tribe in the Iron Age, who settled in the area around 100BC.

Roman Times

The arrival of the Romans in the 1st century AD brought great changes to the region that they called Civitas Atrebates, the capital of which, Calleva Atrebatum, lies close to the village of Silchester. Their urban developments brought a new way of life to Britain: streets and drainage systems, markets and shops, theatres and amphitheatres. As the major population centre in the area, Calleva became an important hub in an emerging road network, with roads radiating out to such places as Dorchester-on-Thames, London, Cirencester and Bath. However, unlike many other towns (which continued to prosper and grow after the Romans left) Calleva was completely abandoned in the late 5th century. Many Roman artefacts from the site can be seen in the museum at Reading.

Dark Ages and the Anglo-Saxon Period

After the departure of the Romans, Anglo-Saxon invaders arrived from Denmark and Northern Germany and moved west up the Thames Valley. During this time the kingdom of Wessex was formed and covered large parts of southern England, including Berkshire and Hampshire, and southwest into Somerset and Dorset. In

AD634 St Birinus brought Christianity to the region that was then under the rule of King Cynegils. The ancient abbey at Abingdon was founded only 40 years later and the building of churches and monasteries followed; elements of Saxon architecture can still be seen in some village churches. Later Viking invaders waged war with the local population over a number of years and recorded some famous victories and losses, including King Alfred's triumph at the Battle of Ashdown.

Norman and Medieval Times

After the Norman Conquest of 1066, the character of the region changed once again. The victorious Normans built castles, the Saxon estates were awarded to loyal Normans and the feudal system was introduced. Twenty years after the Norman invasion the Domesday Book was compiled and gave a detailed picture of Britain. By this time Wallingford had a population of 3000 and Reading about 700, villages prospered, and more and more countryside fell to cultivation and farming.

Recent Times

A growing cloth industry centred on Newbury, Reading and Abingdon brought prosperity to the region. In 1534 Henry VIII broke with Rome and established the Church of England, and two years later the Dissolution of the Monasteries saw the wholesale destruction of many monastic buildings. During the Civil War (1642–48) between King Charles I and Parliament, this area was one of the main battlegrounds. At the time of King George I, road improvements were carried out as a result of the Turnpike Trusts, which initiated the collection of tolls and took on the maintenance of roadways.

King George III re-established Windsor as the main royal residence in 1760. In the early 1800s the Kennet and Avon Canal was built, linking the Westcountry to London and enabling a vastly increased volume of goods to be transported across the country. However, the canal was soon outshone by the arrival of the railways; by 1840 Isambard Kingdom Brunel's famous Great Western Railway had crossed the region. As a result the town of Reading developed into a bustling manufacturing and commercial centre, dominated by the 'three Bs': Bulbs (Sutton Seeds), Biscuits (Huntley and Palmer) and Beer (Simonds Brewery). Today developments progress at a rapid pace, with Reading often being called the 'commercial capital of the Thames Valley'.

APPENDIX 2
Local Geology

The geology of the region tells the story of the seas that once covered southern England and the sediments that were laid down at that time.

It is perhaps easiest to think of the geological structure as a multi-layered cake. The lowest layers are formed of the oldest rocks, the Oxford Clays overlaid with the Kimmeridge and Gault Clays, interspersed with a layer of Jurassic limestone. In the middle is Cretaceous chalk (65–95 million years old), and finally at the top are the more recent layers, such as the Reading Beds, London Clay and Bagshot Sands. Over millions of years this sedimentary 'cake' was raised above sea level. The collision of the European and African continental plates that formed the Alps also caused the 'cake' to ripple and buckle, with a gentle tilt to the southeast. More recently, erosive forces have cut through the layers to reveal the underlying geology.

In the northwest the Oxford Clays are exposed, and the Jurassic limestone layer sandwiched between the clay and sand belts forms a feature known as the Golden Ridge, passing through Longworth and Faringdon to Cumnor on the outskirts of Oxford. In the southeast these clays are buried and the Bagshot Sands emerge at the surface.

In the centre of the region is a wide expanse of chalk, approximately 220m (722ft) thick and formed over 25 million years (it takes around 1000 years to produce just 10mm of chalk). The exposed upper (northern) edge of the chalk layer forms a ridge which runs past White Horse Hill (261m/856ft) near Uffington to the Thames at Goring and then continues along the Chiltern ridge. This sheet of chalk passes south under the Kennet Valley and reappears to form a ridge – the North Hampshire Downs – which includes Walbury Hill (297m/975ft), the highest chalk hill in England. In the east the chalk reappears around Sonning, Henley-on-Thames, Cookham and Maidenhead. This folded layer of chalk also forms the North and South Downs (South Downs from Hampshire and through East and West Sussex; North Downs from the Hamshire/Surrey border through to the White Cliffs of Dover in Kent), and the Purbeck Hills in Dorset. Associated with the chalk are irregular silica concretions, known as flints, which also occur in profusion in the jumbled deposits of weathered chalk known as 'clay-with-flints'. Flint has been widely used as a building material, from the Roman walls at Silchester to many churches, and is a characteristic of the region.

South of the Berkshire Downs, running from Hungerford through Reading to Windsor and the London Basin, the surface is made up of the clays and sands of

The path to Longworth (Walk 7) goes along the limestone layer known as the 'golden ridge'

the Reading, London and Bagshot Beds. A natural process of patchy and irregular hardening within the sandy beds produces boulders of tough sandstone which appear on the surface when the softer sands are eroded. These are the famous sarsens, used in the construction of the Neolithic long barrow at Wayland's Smithy and seen lying in the fields around Ashdown House near Lambourn.

More recently glaciation has played its part, even though the ice sheet never extended south of the line of the River Thames. One of the most dramatic effects on the region was the creation of the Goring Gap and the diversion of the Thames southwards to flow past Reading; originally the river flowed through the Vale of St Albans, past Watford and Hertford. The gap was created when a large glacial lake, which formed over the Oxford area, eroded a line of weakness in the chalk.

APPENDIX 3
Useful Contacts

Tourist Information Offices
Reading
www.readingtourism.org.uk

Faringdon
The Pump House
5 Market Place
Faringdon SN7 7HL
Tel: 01367 242191
www.faringdontowncouncil.org.uk

Henley-on-Thames
King's Arms Barn
King's Road
Henley-on-Thames RG9 2DG
Tel: 01491 578034
www.visithenley-on-thames.co.uk

Newbury
The Granary
Wharf Street
Newbury RG14 5AS
Tel: 01635 30267
www.westberks.gov.uk

Oxford
15–16 Broad Street
Oxford OX1 3AS
Tel: 01865 252200
www.oxford.gov.uk

Swindon
37 Regent Street,
Swindon SN1 1JL
Tel: 01793 530328/466454
www.visitswindon.co.uk

Wantage
The Vale and Downland Museum
Church Street
Wantage OX12 8BL
Tel: 01235 760176
www.wantage.com/museum

Bus Companies
The following bus companies currently
operate in the region:

Arriva Buses
Tel: 01923 682262
www.arriva.co.uk

Cango (Hampshire Council Travel)
Tel: 0845 6024135
www.hants.gov.uk/passengertransport/
cango

Reading/Newbury Buses
Tel: 0118 959 4000 (Reading Buses)
Tel: 01635 567500 (Newbury Buses)
www.reading-buses.co.uk

Stagecoach in Oxfordshire
Tel: 01865 772250
www.stagecoachbus.com/oxfordshire

Stagecoach in Swindon
Tel: 01793 522243
www.stagecoachbus.com/Swindon

Thamesdown Transport
Tel: 01793 428428
www.thamesdown-transport.co.uk

Thames Travel Buses
Tel: 01491 837988
www.thames-travel.co.uk

Local Wildlife Trusts
Berks, Bucks and Oxon Wildlife Trust
The Lodge
1 Armstrong Road
Littlemore OX4 4XT
Tel: 01865 775476
www.bbowt.org.uk

Hampshire and Isle of Wight Wildlife Trust
Beechcroft House
Vicarage Lane
Curdridge SO32 2DP
Tel: 01489 774400
www.hwt.org.uk

Northmoor Trust
Hill Farm
Little Wittenham OX14 4QZ
Tel: 01865 407792
www.northmoortrust.co.uk

Wiltshire Wildlife Trust
Elm Tree Court
Long Street
Devizes SN10 1NJ
Tel: 01380 725670
www.wiltshirewildlife.org

Animal Rescue (injured animals/birds)
If you see any injured animals or birds
while out walking, try contacting:

RSPCA
Tel: 0870 5555999
www.rspca.org.uk

St Tiggywinkles Wildlife Hospital
Tel: 01844 292292
www.sttiggywinkles.org.uk

Areas of Outstanding Natural Beauty
Chilterns AONB
The Lodge
Station Road
Chinnor OX39 4HA
Tel: 01844 355500
www.chilternsaonb.org

North Wessex Downs AONB
Denford Manor
Hungerford RG17 0UN
Tel: 01488 685440
www.northwessexdowns.org.uk

APPENDIX 4
Further Reading

Ackroyd, Peter. *Thames: Sacred River* (Chatto & Windus, 2007)

Corrie, Euan. *Kennet and Avon Canal: From the Thames to Bristol* (Waterways World Ltd, 2002)

Draper, Jo. *Hampshire – the Complete Guide* (The Dovecote Press, 1990)

Goldsack, Paul. *River Thames – in the Footsteps of the Famous* (Bradt, 2003)

Graham, Morris A. *The Vale of White Horse* (Sutton Publishing Ltd, 1993)

Jenkins, Simon. *England's Thousand Best Churches* (Penguin, 1999)

Mills, A.D. *Oxford Dictionary of English Place Names* (Oxford University Press, 2003)

Pevsner, Nikolaus. *The Buildings of England – County Series* (Penguin, various dates)

Sale, Richard. *A Guide to the Chilterns, Marlborough Downs and Oxford* (The Crowood Press Ltd, 1999)

Whitehead, David. *Henley-on-Thames: A History* (Phillimore & Co Ltd, 2007)

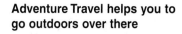

LISTING OF CICERONE GUIDES

BACKPACKING
Backpacker's Britain:
   Vol 1 – Northern England
   Vol 2 – Wales
   Vol 3 – Northern Scotland
   Vol 4 – Southern Highlands
Book of the Bivvy
End to End Trail
National Trails
Three Peaks, Ten Tors

BRITISH CYCLE GUIDES
Border Country Cycle Routes
Cumbria Cycle Way
Lancashire Cycle Way
Lands End to John O'Groats
Rural Rides:
   No 1 – West Surrey
   No 2 – East Surrey
South Lakeland Cycle Rides

CANOE GUIDES
Canoeist's Guide to the North-East

DERBYSHIRE, PEAK DISTRICT, EAST MIDLANDS
High Peak Walks
Historic Walks in Derbyshire
Star Family Walks Peak District and
   South Yorkshire
Walking in Peakland
White Peak Walks:
   Vol 1 – Northern Dales
   Vol 2 – Southern Dales

FOR COLLECTORS OF SUMMITS
Mountains of England & Wales:
   Vol 1 – Wales
   Vol 2 – England
Relative Hills of Britain

IRELAND
Irish Coast to Coast Walk
Irish Coastal Walks
Mountains of Ireland

ISLE OF MAN
Isle of Man Coastal Path
Walking on the Isle of Man

LAKE DISTRICT AND MORECAMBE BAY
Atlas of the English Lakes
Coniston Copper Mines
Cumbria Coastal Way
Cumbria Way and Allerdale Ramble
Great Mountain Days in the
   Lake District
Lake District Anglers' Guide
Lake District Winter Climbs
Roads and Tracks of the Lake District
Rocky Rambler's Wild Walks
Scrambles in the Lake District:
   North
   South
Short Walks in Lakeland:
   Book 1 – South
   Book 2 – North
   Book 3 – West

Tarns of Lakeland:
   Vol 1 – West
   Vol 2 – East
Tour of the Lake District
Walks in Silverdale and
   Arnside
Lakeland Fellranger:
   The Central Fells
   The Mid-Western Fells
   The Near-Eastern Fells
   The Southern Fells

MIDLANDS
Cotswold Way

**NORTHERN ENGLAND
LONG-DISTANCE TRAILS**
Dales Way
Hadrian's Wall Path
Northern Coast to Coast Walk
Pennine Way
Teesdale Way

NORTH-WEST ENGLAND
Family Walks in the
   Forest of Bowland
Historic Walks in Cheshire
Ribble Way
Walker's Guide to the
   Lancaster Canal
Walking in the Forest of Bowland
   and Pendle
Walking in Lancashire
Walks in Lancashire Witch Country
Walks in Ribble Country

**PENNINES AND
NORTH-EAST ENGLAND**
Cleveland Way and Yorkshire
   Wolds Way
Historic Walks in North Yorkshire
North York Moors
South Pennine Walks
Spirit of Hadrian's Wall
Yorkshire Dales – South and West
Walking in County Durham
Walking in Northumberland
Walking in the South Pennines
Walking in the Wolds
Walks in Dales Country
Walks in the Yorkshire Dales
Walks on the North York Moors:
   Books 1 and 2
Waterfall Walks – Teesdale and High
   Pennines
Yorkshire Dales Angler's Guide

SCOTLAND
Ben Nevis and Glen Coe
Border Country
Border Pubs and Inns
Central Highlands
Great Glen Way
Isle of Skye
North to the Cape
Lowther Hills
Pentland Hills

Scotland's Far North
Scotland's Far West
Scotland's Mountain Ridges
Scottish Glens:
   1 – The Cairngorm Glens
   2 – Atholl Glens
   3 – Glens of Rannoch
   4 – Glens of Trossach
   5 – Glens of Argyll
   6 – The Great Glen
Scrambles in Lochaber
Southern Upland Way
Torridon
Walking in the Cairngorms
Walking in the Hebrides
Walking on the Isle of Arran
Walking in the Ochils, Campsie Fells
   and Lomond Hills
Walking in the Orkney and the
   Shetland Isles
Walking the Galloway Hills
Walking the Munros:
   Vol 1 – Southern and Central
   Vol 2 – Northern and Cairngorms
West Highland Way
Winter Climbs – Ben Nevis and
   Glencoe
Winter Climbs – Cairngorms

SOUTHERN ENGLAND
Channel Island Walks
Definitive Guide to Walking
   in London
Exmoor and the Quantocks
Greater Ridgeway
Isles of Scilly
Lea Valley Walk
North Downs Way
South Downs Way
South West Coast Path
Thames Path
Walker's Guide to the Isle of Wight
Walking in Bedfordshire
Walking in Berkshire
Walking in Buckinghamshire
Walking in Dorset
Walking in Kent
Walking in Somerset
Walking in Sussex
Walking in the Thames Valley
Walking on Dartmoor

WALES AND WELSH BORDERS
Ascent of Snowdon
Glyndwr's Way
Hillwalking in Wales:
   Vols 1 and 2
Hillwalking in Snowdonia
Lleyn Peninsula Coastal Path
Pembrokeshire Coastal Path
Ridges of Snowdonia
Scrambles in Snowdonia
Shropshire Hills
Spirit Paths of Wales
Walking Offa's Dyke Path

Walking in Pembrokeshire
Welsh Winter Climbs

AFRICA
Climbing in the Moroccan Anti-Atlas
Kilimanjaro
Trekking in the Atlas Mountains

THE ALPS (Walking and Trekking)
100 Hut Walks in the Alps
Across the Eastern Alps: The E5
Alpine Points of View
Alpine Ski Mountaineering:
    Vol 1 – Western Alps
    Vol 2 – Eastern Alps
Chamonix to Zermatt
Snowshoeing: Techniques and Routes
    in the Western Alps
Tour of Mont Blanc
Tour of Monte Rosa
Tour of the Matterhorn
Walking in the Alps

EASTERN EUROPE
High Tatras
Mountains of Romania
Walking in Hungary

FRANCE, BELGIUM AND LUXEMBOURG
Cathar Way
Ecrins National Park
GR5 Trail
GR20 Corsica
Mont Blanc Walks
Robert Louis Stevenson Trail
Rock Climbs Belgium and
    Luxembourg
Tour of the Oisans: The GR54
Tour of the Vanoise
Trekking in the Vosges and Jura
Vanoise Ski Touring
Walking in the Cathar Region
Walking in the Cevennes
Walking in the Dordogne
Walking in the Haute Savoie:
    Vol 1 – North
    Vol 2 – South
Walking in the Languedoc
Walking in Provence
Walking in the Tarentaise and
    Beaufortain Alps
Walking on Corsica
Walking the French Gorges
Walks in Volcano Country

GERMANY AND AUSTRIA
Germany's Romantic Road
King Ludwig Way
Klettersteig – Scrambles in
    Northern Limestone Alps
Mountain Walking in Austria
Trekking in the Stubai Alps
Trekking in the Zillertal Alps
Walking in the Bavarian Alps
Walking in the Harz Mountains
Walking in the Salzkammergut
Walking the River Rhine Trail

HIMALAYAS – NEPAL, INDIA, TIBET
Annapurna
Bhutan
Everest
Garhwal & Kumaon
Kangchenjunga
Langtang, Gosainkund and
    Helambu
Manaslu
Mount Kailash Trek

ITALY
Central Apennines of Italy
Gran Paradiso
Italian Rock
Shorter Walks in the Dolomites
Through the Italian Alps: the GTA
Trekking in the Apennines
Treks in the Dolomites
Via Ferratas of the Italian
    Dolomites:
    Vols 1 and 2
Walking in Sicily
Walking in the Central Italian Alps
Walking in the Dolomites
Walking in Tuscany

NORTH AMERICA
Grand Canyon and American South
    West
John Muir Trail
Walking in British Columbia

OTHER MEDITERRANEAN COUNTRIES
Climbs and Treks in the Ala Dag
    (Turkey)
Crete: the White Mountains
High Mountains of Crete
Jordan – Walks, Treks, Caves etc.
Mountains of Greece
Treks and Climbs Wadi Rum, Jordan
Walking in Malta
Walking in Western Crete

PYRENEES AND FRANCE/SPAIN
Canyoning in Southern Europe
GR10 Trail: Through the
    French Pyrenees
Mountains of Andorra
Rock Climbs in the Pyrenees
Pyrenean Haute Route
Pyrenees – World's Mountain Range
    Guide
Through the Spanish Pyrenees: the
    GR11
Walks and Climbs in the Pyrenees
Way of St James – France
Way of St James – Spain

SCANDINAVIA
Pilgrim Road to Nidaros
    (St Olav's Way)
Walking in Norway

SLOVENIA, CROATIA AND MONTENEGRO
Julian Alps of Slovenia
Mountains of Montenegro
Walking in Croatia

SOUTH AMERICA
Aconcagua

SPAIN AND PORTUGAL
Costa Blanca Walks:
    Vol 1 – West
    Vol 2 – East
Mountains of Central Spain
Walks and Climbs in the Picos
    d'Europa
Via de la Plata (Seville to Santiago)
Walking in the Algarve
Walking in the Canary Islands:
    Vol 1 – West
    Vol 2 – East
Walking in the Cordillera Cantabrica
Walking the GR7 in Andalucia
Walking in Madeira
Walking in Mallorca
Walking in the Sierra Nevada

SWITZERLAND
Alpine Pass Route
Bernese Alps
Central Switzerland
Tour of the Jungfrau Region
Walking in Ticino
Walking in the Valais
Walks in the Engadine

INTERNATIONAL CYCLE GUIDES
Cycle Touring in France
Cycle Touring in Spain
Cycle Touring in Switzerland
Cycling in the French Alps
Cycling the River Loire – The Way
    of St Martin
Danube Cycle Way
Way of St James – Le Puy to Santiago

MINI GUIDES
Avalanche!
Navigating with GPS
Navigation
First Aid and Wilderness Medicine
Snow

TECHNIQUES AND EDUCATION
Adventure Alternative
Beyond Adventure
Hillwalker's Guide to Mountaineering
Hillwalker's Manual
Map and Compass
Mountain Weather
Moveable Feasts
Outdoor Photography
Rock Climbing
Snow and Ice
Sport Climbing

For full and up-to-date information on
our ever-expanding list of guides,
please check our website:
www.cicerone.co.uk.

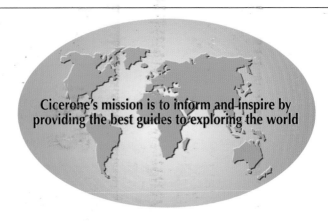

Cicerone's mission is to inform and inspire by
providing the best guides to exploring the world

Since its foundation over 30 years ago, Cicerone has specialised in
publishing guidebooks and has built a reputation for quality and reliability.
It now publishes nearly 300 guides to the major destinations for outdoor
enthusiasts, including Europe, UK and the rest of the world.

Written by leading and committed specialists, Cicerone guides are
recognised as the most authoritative. They are full of information, maps and
illustrations so that the user can plan and complete a successful and safe
trip or expedition – be it a long face climb, a walk over Lakeland fells, an
alpine traverse, a Himalayan trek or a ramble in the countryside.

With a thorough introduction to assist planning, clear diagrams, maps and
colour photographs to illustrate the terrain and route, and accurate and
detailed text, Cicerone guides are designed for ease of use and access to
the information.

If the facts on the ground change, or there is any aspect of a guide that you
think we can improve, we are always delighted to hear from you.

Cicerone Press
2 Police Square Milnthorpe Cumbria LA7 7PY
Tel: 015395 62069 Fax: 015395 63417
info@cicerone.co.uk www.cicerone.co.uk

CICERONE